THE *Essence* OF SETTERS

*An In-depth
Study of the
Four Setters*

MARSHA HALL BROWN

THE  *Essence* OF SETTERS

*An In-depth
Study of the
Four Setters*

MARSHA HALL BROWN

*With Original Art and Illustrations
by
Patricia J. Detmold*

*With Contributions by:
Patricia Brigden, Dawn Ferguson, Peter A. Frost,
Shelley P. LeBlanc and Joseph A. LeBlanc,
John Savory, and Dennis J. Sporre*

Published by Doral Publishing, Sun City, Arizona
Printed in the United States of America.

Interior Design by The Printed Page
Cover Design by 1106 Design
Cover illustration by Patricia J. Detmold

Library of Congress Card Number: 2001098697
ISBN: 0-944875-55-6

Publisher's Cataloging-in-Publication
(Provided by Quality Books, Inc.)

Brown, Marsha Hall.
    The essence of setters : a study of the English
  Gordon, Irish and Red and White setters. -- 1st ed.
    p. cm.
    Includes bibliographical references and index.
    LCCN 2001098697
    ISBN 0-944875-55-6

    1. Setters (Dogs)   I. Title.

SF429.S5B76 2002   636.752'6
                                    QBI01-201544

Introducing the Author

$\mathcal{B}$ecause of the long and enduring relationship we've shared through the wonderful world of dog shows, it gives me great pleasure to be asked to write the introduction to Marsha Hall Brown's definitive work on Setters. There are many parallels in our lives beginning with the fact that we first competed against each other in the Children's Handling Class at Windham County, Connecticut in 1949. It was Marsha's first win and my first time in the ring. After we "met" a year later as pen-pals through the Girl Scouts' *American Girl Magazine*, we began spending time together at shows in New England. Our parents, the Halls and the Colemans took pleasure in sharing this sport of dogs with their children, and they encouraged us to persevere in the breed ring at a time when very few young people were considered serious competitors. Later, our parents took pride in sharing our accomplishments as breeders and judges.

Marsha's contributions in the fields of writing and education have brought her national recognition. From her beginning with *Popular Dogs Magazine* to breed columnist for the The *American Kennel Gazette* to the publishing of *The Junior Showmanship Handbook* (co-authored with her sister) to columnist for *Dog News* and now *The Essence of Setters*, she has had an impact on our sport. Yet, my particular admiration for Marsha centers around her passion for excellence in education.

After we had been out of touch with each other for nearly twenty years, our paths crossed again in California in 1977. This meeting of two Yankee gals living far away from "home" led to our working together to form the San Francisco Bay Area Judges Workshop, one of the first regional judges' study groups in the United States.

In recent years Marsha's enthusiasm for her career as a college professor of Speech Communication and Rhetorical Studies in

Orange County, California has limited her time spent at shows, yet it has at the same time has enhanced the contributions she has made in her numerous lectures and seminars on her first loves, English Setters and Junior Showmanship.

Best of all, my friend has led a life of diverse interests and abilities. Marsha has been an active volunteer in the Girl Scouts and Boy Scouts, has taught swimming and water safety, published original research on American Women's Studies, and has kept close to her roots on Nantucket Island, Massachusetts. Married to her high school sweetheart for forty five years, Marsha with her husband Bob have raised three children and are proud grandparents. She is, indeed, a bright and fun-loving person and I am proud to call her my loyal friend.

Lydia Coleman Hutchinson
Wolfpit Cairns, Middletown, Maryland

About the Illustrator

*P*ATRICIA J. DETMOLD grew up in Eastern Canada where her parents who immigrated from England, bred, raised and showed English Cockers and English Setters. Pat first proved her excellence in the ring as a handler by winning Children's Handling Classes at Berwick, Nova Scotia, Halifax, and Montreal in the 1940's. She exhibited her family's Spruce setters to many championships in both Canada and the United States and she trained for both Obedience and Field. After graduation from the Congregation de Notre Dame Convent with private studies with one of the nuns who was herself an artist, Pat studied at the Canadian School of Commercial Art in Montreal, worked as an artist for several corporations and soon became a freelance artist specializing in wildlife and animal portraiture. In 1961 Pat Detmold's entry at the Society of Animal Artists Spotlight Show in New York City entitled, *Bird Dog*, was the Jury Selection. Moving to the United States in 1964, Pat's pure-bred dog portraits in pastels, watercolor and oil were in demand initially by setter fanciers. Since then her commissions have included many breeds of dogs, horses and cats. Her work has been published in calendars, books and a variety of dog publications and her dog art for show trophies has become collector items. Today, Pat, who breeds and shows English Cockers under the Sprucerun prefix has a private studio in Flemington, New Jersey.

Patricia Detmold and her Spruce Setters with Canada's Governor General Mr. Massey in 1957 at the United States

About the Editor

*T*HOMAS W. HALL, JR. was the only member of the Hall family to pursue other interests when the station wagon left for dog shows. After graduation from Dartmouth, Tom became a Naval Officer, pursued a career in teaching high school English and Latin, and has for many years been in demand as a musician and entertainer. Today he is a minister, Biblical scholar and professional book editor and lives in Foster, Rhode Island.

Tom Hall, Jr. poses here with the first show bred setter to visit Stone Gables in 1940. The bitch was an English import owned by Tom's uncle, Gordon LeBaron Farrier of Nantucket, Massachusetts.

Introducing the Contributors

Patricia Brigden
Caterham, Surrey, England

Author of the only book devoted to Irish Red and White Setters, Patricia Brigden began as an owner and exhibitor of Autumnwood Irish Setters many years before she became involved in the re-establishment of the Red and White Setter in the early 1980's in England. She is a breeder, exhibitor and championship show judge. Her painstaking research on the origins and the revival of the Red and White provides today's setter fancier with essential information. Mrs. Brigden, a retired public utility manager, spends leisure time gardening, listening to music and traveling.

Dawn Ferguson
Freeman's Reach, New South Wales, Australia

Although an Australian Cattle Dog was her first friend and protector, Mrs. Ferguson also had Kelpies, Stumpy Tails, Irish Setters, and German Shepherds, and has bred Cockers (English) and Dobermans. She established Warchant in 1960, becoming a major breeder of Gordon Setters. Dawn created a breeding plan, brought in imports to diversify the breeding base, and has studied the breed by traveling and judging in many countries. Licensed for all sporting breeds, Dawn has judged at both the Gordon and English Setter Nationals in the United States, and is an Honorary Member of The Gordon Setter Club of America. A retired elementary school teacher, she is also an artist in various media and a collector of antiques and dog memorabilia.

Peter A. Frost
Melbourne, Victoria, Australia

Known to many Irish Setter fanciers as the judge at the National Specialty in St. Louis, Peter Frost began breeding and exhibiting under the prefix, Rosslare, in 1972. He is licensed for All Sporting, All Hounds and All Terriers. A skilled craftsman in building period antique reproductions, he is also an avid horse-racing fan. Professionally, Peter teaches senior math and calculus courses in the high school where he is also director of the study of Classics.

Shelley P. LeBlanc and Joseph A. LeBlanc
Little Falls, Minnesota

The LeBlancs are professional field trainers specializing in Setters and Pointers at their Rice Creek Kennels and game preserve. Shelley has bred and handled many Gordon Setters to dual titles since 1982 and has also trained her dogs in Obedience. On the support staff at the Minnesota State Patrol Cadet School and head coach of the Little Falls High School Gymnastics team, Shelley enjoys horseback riding, hunting and camping with her family. Joseph owns and manages the 1700 acre shooting preserve and has been active as a breeder of German Shorthaired Pointers, a field trainer, exhibitor and judge for twenty-five years. He is also an avid hunter, fisherman and chess player.

John Savory
Keswick, Virginia

Since 1962 John Savory has bred Dunholm Irish Setters. A licensed judge of international experience, he also breeds Rhodesian Ridgebacks and is a lecturer on Irish Setters. John is a competitive runner, opera buff, and golfer. Professionally, he is a Professor of Pathology, Biochemistry and Molecular Genetics and Director of the Clinical Laboratories at the University of Virginia.

Dennis J. Sporre
Greensboro, North Carolina

A former breeder and exhibitor of champion Irish Setters, a licensed judge of All Setters, an officer of the Irish Setter Club of America, and Dog Writer of the Year recipient for his series published in the Irish Setter *Memo*, Dennis Sporre has recently retired from a thirty year academic career. He was a professor, department chair, and most recently, Academic Dean at Ball State University. Dennis an award winning author of eleven books on the arts and cultural history.

Dedication

*T*his book is dedicated to the men and women in the sport of dogs who took the time, the interest and the patience to share with me their knowledge and their understanding of Setters. As I write this manuscript, I am reminded of their words and deeds, and I am forever grateful for the unique privilege of their guidance and friendship.

Davis Tuck talked about the significance of pedigrees and explained the value of a dog like Raff despite the color and markings. He explained the principle of the third generation goal.

Teddy Hayes, the famous judge who began as the groomer for Dr. Mitten's Happy Valley Kennels, created an oral exam for me and required that I discuss the balance of angulation in English Setters as key to quality.

John Downs explained the temperament of Irish Setters and gave advice on how to keep an Irish interested in the show ring by using the secret "pebble method."

W. Enos Phillips took me through the Pointer and Beagle kennel at Harbor Hill. He was dressed for the lesson in riding trousers and carried a riding crop which he used to point out the details of how a dog had to be built to serve a purpose. His kennel man moved selected dogs so Mr. Phillips could explain pointer style and how the set and carriage of the tail made the dog a pointer and nothing else.

John Stocker of Yorkley fame explained how to sort a ring of dogs and how to employ a technique of judging to find what you had to know. I re-read his letters so that I can remember his excellence as a Setter judge.

Ted Eldredge talked to me of dog care and management as essential factors to Setter temperament. His letters of encouragement and advice on judging are my treasures.

Catherine Bede Maxwell, (the indominable Maxie) helped me put the bits and pieces of my dog information together in my head so that I could see an ideal of the breed—first a silhouette and then the details. She insisted on a new level of understanding that included the study of many other sporting breeds and what they were bred to do.

Graeme Lack, the importer of the famous Gordon Setter Sutherland Hallmark into Australia, taught me that the heated discussion over every detail of the Setter standards should be a common occurrence among friends and colleagues.

Alex Price of Whernside English and Irish Setter fame, who was also an all-breed international judge, helped me understand and experience the excellence of Setters in Australia, and remember that the dogs in the United States could yield only part of the total knowledge of the breeds.

Harold Sydney cared so much about Gordons that he always stayed for the Group even at a time when Gordons would rarely be considered for placement. He wanted Gordons to be seen and understood. He taught me patience and described the different characteristics that made Gordon Setters unique.

Muriel Clement trusted me with handling her foundation bitch, Bonny, at the Pawtucket show. After that we saw each other often, and she wanted me to know about the coats of Gordons and why they needed to be shiny black.

Sally Howe brought a new joy to the setter circle—at once a prankster with a wild sense of humor and a hard working and dedicated breeder who had the confidence in her Clariho dogs to hand them to her young daughters to campaign.

George Brodie would race up our long driveway at Stone Gables in his maroon Porsche to stop and have coffee and pie and talk dogs. He described the great Irish that we had never seen. Later at shows he would explain the difficulty of placements after "first" and the methods he used to establish his decision.

Elsworth Howell was my most loyal friend and teacher. He encouraged my involvement in English Setters from the very beginning and he provided unlimited opportunities for me to learn and succeed. His letter to me about the significance of the written standard is framed and is always over my desk where I can see it and think of his life of contributions to Setters.

Marsha Hall Brown

Top row: Elsworth Howell and C. Bede Maxwell, W. Enos Phillips and Lady Helen Phillips. Middle Row: Alex Price, Davis Tuck. Bottom Row: Ted Eldredge, Graeme Lack

Acknowledgments

$\mathcal{T}$he response to my requests for information and photos for this book has been a memorable and heartening experience. The old song's reminder to "make new friends and keep the old, one is silver and the other gold" has proven to be true. These treasured friends have searched their collections for photos that have helped me identify the essence of each breed and thus tell the setter story. Many photos are significant in that they have never been published before. Other photos depict setter men and women of the past who must never be forgotten. And still others show the breeds of setters as they exist today. I wish to thank all who have contributed to this book. Your time and efforts are appreciated and will always be remembered.

My special thanks go to individuals who have made significant contributions of time and expertise: John Lawreck, Joyce Nilsen, Charles Oldham, Jeannette Brady Shields, Virginia Tuck Hall, Canon Patrick Doherty, Paula McAteer, Charles Herendeen, Anne Rogers Clark, Dean and Jane Matteson, Susan DeSilva, Richard Knoster, Mary Ann Samuelson, Anne Eldredge Mateer, Carl Sillman, Angie Sparkes and John Nielsen. Instrumental in helping me obtain noteworthy art of setters for reproduction in this book were James Crowley of the American Kennel Club, Ray Steadman of Wilton House representing the Earl of Pembroke, Martin Durrant staff member of the Victoria and Albert Museum in London, staff members of the Staatliche; Museum in Berlin, Germany, the staff at the Metropolitan Museum in New York, Jim O'Callaghan and Edwina Mulvany at the Irish National Museum in Dublin, and Clive Rex Alexander for giving me permission to reproduce the painting of *The Scottish Game Keeper*.

Robert Remeika, and Bob Brown provided photographic expertise, Jackie Kessler has consistently offered advice on methods of research and patiently listened to my frustrations and tales of woe, and John Kessler ferreted out information that no one else was able to find. I also thank the Kesslers for the loan of their mezzotint, "*Setters*," by G. Moorland. Rebec Pusey Riggs provided me with a network of dog fanciers' e-mail addresses that was critical to my research. Bill and Marvin (Lovey) Trotter have made their *English Setter Breeder of the Year Scrapbook* available to me for information and for one-of-a-kind photos of the past.

I now know why writers thank their assistants. For without my right hand person, the always cheerful and superbly competent, Mary Hargett, this book would never have become a reality.

Finally, my profound appreciation to the publisher of this book, Dr. Alvin Grossman, for inviting me to take on this important challenge and for having the patience in waiting for the final manuscript.

To all friends old and new, my grateful thanks.

Marsha Hall Brown

Preface

$\mathcal{D}$own through the years many people have written about setters. Among them have been scholars, diplomats, sportsmen, scientists, judges and breeders of great dogs. Certainly, I am none of these. Therefore, when the publisher of this book, Dr. Alvin Grossman, approached me with the suggestion that I write a book on setters, I was not at all sure that I was up to such a serious challenge. After all, my first two books were on Junior Showmanship, and during those processes my friend and publisher, the late Elsworth Howell had both held and guided my hand all the way. After getting over the inevitable ego boost resulting from the invitation to write about the breeds I loved most, I began to wonder about his reasons: "Why me?" Al Grossman and I were judging colleagues who had studied together, and he was familiar with the collection of slides I had collected to illustrate the presentations I had given on the three setter breeds. But those were *his* reasons. I had to ask myself what I could offer a reader.

Although I had, indeed, been a breeder, a licensed handler and was now a judge, I was hardly an expert who has devoted a lifetime to dogs and dog shows. Still, I had never been satisfied with the slides as illustrations of the breeds I sought to explain. Dog show photographs, even of superb dogs, do not often provide appropriate examples of the standards. I could not do justice to the magnificent setters I have known using photos cluttered with bystanders, trophies, flowers, signs and, alas all too often, a handler who is holding the head and tail aloft, destroying every element of the dog's natural balance and symmetry. Nor did I want to present photos that might be seen as advertisements for any person, kennel or group of dogs. And I was often frustrated to find, when presenting the slides as an illustration of breed type or breed anatomy, that members of the audience were more interested in "what dog?" "what judge?" and "what show?"

Further, I was aware that today setter people tend to be more involved with show statistics, records, and strategy than with setter standards and setter type. I had also come to recognize that on many occasions when a club in the United States asks for a critique of the entry, what they really expect are positive comments to confirm the excellent work all the breeders are doing.

On the other hand, I felt some anxiety about raising what might prove to be divisive issues. Of even greater concern was the prospect of leaving out the "fourth setter"—the Irish Red and White about which I knew very little aside from judging the breed on one occasion. Not only did I lack pictures, I didn't know a single person who owned a Red and White. And above all I would have to determine what my purpose would be in writing this book.

But at precisely that point the project became more plausible. I began to recall an oft-repeated concern from my mentors in the world of setters. "I came from Ireland," Alec Pelan had told me. "An Irish is not supposed to look like an English." Anthony Miller, the owner of the famous Ch. Sharoc Dolly Madison would shake his head politely but firmly and tell me that a Gordon head does not belong on an English. Then I thought of Maxie's lecture in which she argued, "Each setter is in its own right a distinctive breed, different in heritage, habit, anatomy." I remembered the letter from John Stocker about the importance of the *individual* setter standards. Thelma Brown in her lectures and in her book explained that to evaluate any breed it is essential to have a silhouette of the breed firmly fixed in the mind. And finally, I remembered that it was Elsworth Howell himself who had sent me the seed money for the slide project, asking that I volunteer my time to speak to others on the differences between the setters—the differences that some judges, breeders, and handlers often failed to understand. At last I had identified a good reason for writing the book: to explain and describe what each breed must look like and how they differed from one another.

I began my research using the books left to me by my father and his hunting partner, Walton Smith, and some very old dog books lent to me by friends. Then I studied the standards that have been obtained in different times and different countries. By letter and e-mail I inquired around the country and much of the world, and I discussed with friends old and new what my project was all about. Seven experts on setters came forward to contribute to this book. They have been introduced on a previous page. I returned to research using a more modern collection of books, magazines, newsletters, yearbooks, and personal letters—some of which I carried with me from Rhode Island to New Jersey to New York State to Northern California and to Southern California. A survey I conducted among new setter judges yielded common questions and similar needs for information. Then I talked to eight setter specialists whom I have greatly respected for many years, and each offered unique suggestions and comments that have helped me see each breed as it was, as it is now, and as it should be.

In order to provide the reader with illustrations, I invited Patricia Detmold to create paintings and drawings that as closely as possible represented the ideal examples of each of the breeds as described in the standards. I also began a search for photographs that would capture the essence of the setter breeds rather than provide a selection of famous dogs sprinkled throughout a chapter. This selection process was extremely frustrating, for not only were pictures of Red and Whites scarce, but the photographs of Gordon Setters too often proved to be either a clear picture with the wrong shaped dog or a type-correct dog on a dark background. I tried in all ways possible to present dogs separate from owners, judges and handlers so that the viewer would concentrate on the dog. I did make exceptions, however, and used photographs including people when they and the dogs were not from The United States. One further exception was necessary in the case of Gordon Setters when it was impossible to erase a background. Nevertheless I was surprised and gratified by some of the rare photos sent to me by fanciers near and far. And I am very pleased to present a number of extraordinary photos showing the various breeds of setters in the field.

More than ever before I have come to realize the singular importance of the standards and the responsibility each of us has in learning and following the standard as it is written—not as we would like it to be. While not an expert on setters, I am a serious student of the breeds, and I feel a sense of responsibility to share with others the knowledge I have been honored to receive from those so generous to spend time with me during my life in dogs.

Marsha Hall Brown

Contents

1 | Origins of Setters

*W*hen we look upon the setters of today—four separate breeds with four separate standards—we see each with its own unique beauty. This beauty is made up of the in-depth characteristics labeled by the dog sport as *type*. We are familiar with this, we judge it, we derive enjoyment from observing it, and at home we love the look of the dog before us in part because it is aesthetically pleasing. But how the present day breeds of setters became diverse, with each possessing its own type, is a process that has taken place over time and in different countries. To be sure, much of that history derives from documented information; but lack of records, doubtful memories and opinions, and sheer conjecture have combined to render the story neither complete nor objective. In addition, it must be acknowledged that setters generic and setters specific are the result of pragmatic trial and error crossings by the breeders of the past who had one clear goal: to establish a hunting dog that would be durable, trainable, and capable of finding birds.

For the reader it may be disquieting to learn about the "new blood" introduced to a line whether it came from spaniel, setter, pointer, or even dogs outside the group now referred to as Sporting. Although such notions interfere with the pure-bred view of today, our reluctance to accept that the practice of out-crossing went on for over two hundred years and continued even after the dog show and breed standards were in place, is myopic. Not only does it prevent us from appreciating the work and skill of the ancient breeders, but it limits our understanding of the language and inferences in the standards.

1

This chapter will offer a brief history of the setters and will include ancient origins, the era of early dog shows and the creation of breed standards, and setters in The United States.

C. Bede Maxwell describes the origins and diversity of setters this way: "The English is basically a spaniel. The Irish is basically a scent hound. The Gordon partakes of both groupings." In this overview she provides the reader with a way of visualizing how these breeds differ. The Irish stands tall and upright, built for more speed with a slight arch over the loin that was even more obvious in past times. The English has the coat patterns and coat texture akin to the spaniel, with a comely expression reminiscent of the larger spaniels, and with a lower stationed work pattern requiring a level topline. The Gordon, similar to the English in outline, top line and work pattern, is the setter of the most substance and carries the red (or tan) coloring of the Irish and the black that was part of the English color inheritance.

But what of the Irish Red and White? Until the recent arousal of interest in this ancient yet modern-made breed, the reader of setter history apparently skipped over the numerous references to white setters with red patches. (See color plates 9, 10, and 11). The descriptions of red and white setters evidently did not hold interest for Gordon fanciers; the red patches on a white setter were considered a fault to English fanciers; and Irish fanciers, who had been trying to get rid of any trace of

white on their dogs for over a hundred years, did not want to read about the "stain of the past." In fact, none of the modern setter books in the United States identifies the Irish Red and White as a breed. And while Mrs. Maxwell acknowledged that the Irish Setter, *may* be the most ancient of the setters and that the original color was white with red, she never discussed The Red and White as in later times being separate or different in shape and form from the "self-coloured" Irish Setter.

Ancient Origins

Every writer consulted on the subject of setters has a slightly different point of view when explaining the origins of these breeds. But the recent book by Gilbert Leighton-Boyce published in 1985 shows a depth and breadth of research not offered before. He begins by tracing the sport of fowling in which wild birds are taken for food and continues by describing such variations as the use of hawks, shooting with arrows and the use of fixed and mobile nets. He identifies references to the dogs used in conjunction with the taking of birds. The first documentation was from the *Bayeux Tapestry* in which are shown two small hawking dogs, one red and the other tan, being taken from England by Harold's party as a gift to William of Normandy in the 11th Century[1]. These dogs would not merit interest but for the fact that very similar dogs are also shown in greater detail in the Devonshire Hunt Tapestry *Falconry*. Dated in the 1400's, this work shows one dog in particular alert to the work of the hunting party that includes ladies in the finest of court hunting dresses and head coverings. (see color plate 1).

Chronology of Noted Writers

The following list of frequently quoted writers is offered as an aid to readers who wish to keep the research on the setters in context such as historical periods, writers as contemporaries, and the emergence of setter differences. All these writers were published in English except for DeFoix and Caius whose works were later translated into English.

Author	Nom-de-plume	Year of Publication
Gaston De Foix		1406
Johannes Caius		1576
George Tuberville		1576
Gervase Markham		1621
Sydenham Edwards		1801
Mr. H.H. Dixon of Carlisle	The Druid	1865
Rev. Hely Hutchinson	Sixty One	1866
Edward Laverack		1872
Rev. Thomas Pearce	Idstone	1872
John Henry Walsh, MD	Stonehenge	1885
Rawdon Lee		1893
James Watson		1909
Freeman Lloyd		1931
M. Ingle Bepler		1937
C. Bede Maxwell		1972
Gilbert Leighton-Boyce		1985

Since both these early renderings were woven in Europe and depict clearly the work pattern of the setter that Gaston DeFoix calls *coucher*—a dog that goes down in a set position— and since DeFoix describes and illustrates a dog that sets to game in France,[2] it suggests that the setter originated in France or elsewhere in Europe. Hans Bols writing in 1582 includes an illustration that shows a white setter fixed on partridges and comments that there is a clear difference between the spaniel and the setter[3] Further evidence that may suggest an important French connection is a letter written in French and English from Lord Warwick to his brother, Robert Dudley in which he says, "I will send you the best setter in France."[4] Another gift, documented in 1624, was a setting dog given to James I of England from Louis XIII of France.[5] W. Enos Phillips in *The True Pointer*[6] explains that the large sporting kennels in France all kept setters, and these dogs had either come with the Romans or had originated in Spain and then France. The result of this setter development may be seen at the Chateau de Chantilly, which was built in 1719, where setters had their own kennel buildings separate from the pointers and the harriers. Phillips, Rawdon Lee[7] and Vero Shaw[8] also place the setter which is described in texts as the English Setter, as an established hunting breed in France prior to the sixteenth century. Also of interest are the indications in the literature that these setters in France were black and white, red and white, and black, tan and white[9]. From England, Caius in 1576 records in his book, *Of English Dogges* the "marble-blewe" as a new kind of setter from France. Other facts that point to setter origins in France and other parts of Europe come from DeFoix, who mentions the small bedecked hunting hounds that were white flecked with mottlings of black[10]. Interpretations from later writers suggest that the designation hound is a generic term for dog and that bedecked refers to a dog that is "furnished" or coated. Phillips identifies paintings in the Louvre by Francois Desportes that depict setters in the seventeenth century, and many of them are black and white.[11] He also states, "I believe that the setter is a very old breed, brought to a high state of

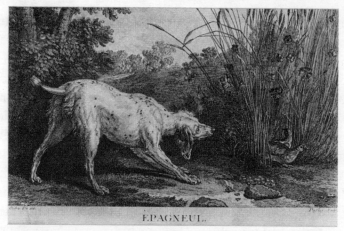

English Setter type labeled as Epagneul (Spaniel) by the artist Jean Babtiste Oudrey. (France)

perfection in France, brought to Scotland along the main water route of travel and from there was distributed to the other parts of Britain[12]." At the Getty Museum in Los Angeles hangs a portrait by Pompeo Batoni (1773) of John Talbot with his black and white setter. The dog has a beautifully chiseled headpiece, low ear set, and feathering on its legs and tail and is described as either a French or Italian Setter. It is thus documented that the early setters of France had the colors and patterns necessary to produce for future generations the specific colors for each of the setter breeds. All writers have alluded to the spaniel, thought to have been the progenitor of the setter, as a dog originating in Spain. But no documentation exists to support this. In fact, Leighton-Boyce and Phillips suggest that spaniel, like the term hound, probably referred to dogs in general in many contexts of the literature. Certainly the dog that Oudrey labels as Epagneul is in all details and type a setter. [13] (see illustration) A final thought on the French origin of setters must include the discussion by Rawdon Lee and Freeman Lloyd, of the introduction of pointers to England. Both agree that pointers arrived in England about 1730 at a time when shooting flying had become a sport. Yet by that time the English Setter was clearly a "tribe of its own" and if there had been a pointer ancestor of the setter, as many claim, it would have had to come much earlier—and in France, where the pointer had been known for a very long time. The precise origins of the setter breeds will never be established, but certainly England was the land where the setter known to us today as the English Setter was developed and nurtured.

The English Setter, it therefore seems, has its origins in the large spaniels sometimes referred to as Land Spaniels. This is certainly plausible when color patterns, coat texture, and general body type is considered. The work pattern of the setter described by Caius and Markham,[14] and which is still with us today, no doubt had to be altered from the spaniels that barked and flushed to the setters that crept and then crouched in silence. Mrs. Maxwell describes it as part way "between the stealth of the primitive dog and the posture of the Lions at Trafalgar Square." The work of the setter was also subject to change: first the net and then the falcons and hawks and finally the gun. Some writers suggest that the drop for the net may be one explanation but that when nets were no longer used the setting position was effective in getting a dog to stop without running into the covey. By the time shooting flying was introduced into England, the English Setter had been long established. Along with the hunting hounds, they were kept in large numbers on estates and hunting preserves and continued to be crossed with other setters to obtain the finest performance in hunting small game.[15] James Watson in his very detailed accounts of setters in *The Dog Book* describes the various kennels in different areas of Great Britain that were identified by the names of the owner or the place.[16] The strains of setters that were kept during the late 1700's and all of the 1800's had changed from the earlier dogs to reflect the owner's preference not only for hunting style and later for field trial ability, but also for aesthetic characteristics. Written descriptions and paintings of English Setters are numerous and show that the head pieces in particular had become very beautiful. Although these large kennels did establish unique strains, the breeding base of English Setters was large, and owners who often hunted together or who leased adjoining hunting properties in Ireland and Scotland surely used one another's lines and occasionally purchased dogs from each other.

Examples of these strains are worthy of mention for they are part of the genetic pool that would influence all the setter breeds as they were exported to The United States. Most importantly, there is first hand documentation offered by Edward Laverack as to the structure, characteristics and color of the English Setters as he saw them in the field and show in Great Britain and Ireland. The following notations about the kennels during the 1800's by Laverack are taken directly from his book, *The Setters*, published in London in 1872 and presented here in a shortened version.

The Naworth Castle and Featherstone Castle Breed:
Big, heavy, great profusion of coat—sort and silky, strong. A tuft of long silky hair on the crest of the head, liver or liver and white. Some went to Ireland.

Lord Lovat's Breed Invernesshire:
Great powers of endurance, kept for utility not show, black, white and tan. One of the best kennels in the North.

The Earl of Southesk's Breed:
Black, white and tan. Fine, strong animals, round barrelled and well feathered. Sometimes slack in the loins but staunch dogs.

The Earl of Seafield's Breed Invernesshire:
Black, white and tan; lemon, orange and white. A pure and beautiful breed, heads short. Beautiful like large toy spaniels, good hunters, easily broken. Objectionable upright shoulders and straight hindquarters.

Lord Ossulston's and Earl of Tankerville's Breed Northumberland:
Jet black, beautiful, powerful with endurance, good retrievers, long and low with light heads, powerful in the forehand, capital feet. Silky coat not in profusion, staunch.

The Llanedloes (Welsh) Breed:
Chalk white, soft and silky coat, adapted to Wales. Also
jet black, hardy enduring on steep hill-sides.

The Russian Setter:
White, lemon and white, liver and white, black and
white. Little known but I have seen them. One was
buried in coat, long floss, silky texture. High courage
and handsome. Obstinate, wilful, eyes completely con-
cealed by hair.[17]

Although the above first person critique is instructional
even for today's reader, it is to Laverack that we owe the even
greater contribution of publishing an explanation of the standard that became an essential guide to the new owners of
setters as the dogs were scattered to new lands.[18] Any contemporary reader would understand the descriptive phrasing
applied to the setter of one hundred and thirty years ago
because it is in essence what we use today. "The ears set low on
the head and flat to the cheeks. A prick eared dog is unsightly.
The shoulders I consider one of the most important parts of the
setter. They should be oblique, the more so the better. (And in a
foot note Laverack continues), 'My greatest object has been to
obtain power and strength in the forequarters.' The back short.
(and he explains it) short above and long below where the
power of stroke, spring, or leverage (come from). The setter
cannot have too much coat for me …the quality of coat is a
great desideratum, and denotes high breeding."[19]

Laverack's conclusion offered a further description of the
dog of great endurance: "Fast, bold, and free, carrying his head
up, whip or feather his stern well in his gallop…and on his
point as rigid and motionless as a statue." [20] These were the
dogs that American sportsmen wanted and these were the
dogs that the Australians associated with what was good
about England. And although the main export of English Setters to places abroad was for the sport in the field, it would be
only two years after Laverack published his book that dog
shows would commence in the United States and bring about a
whole new reason for owning setters.

The first shows in the United States were for Pointers and Setters only, and the classes they offered focused on imported dogs, although there were classes for native setters. In addition, the sires and dams listed were often of another "kind" of setter and the color and style of the dog entered determined its breed. [21] Shows and field trials for the most part remained a leisure activity of the affluent and great kennels both in size and in accomplishment were established in the Northeast especially in the area between Boston and Philadelphia. While native setters and the progeny of the imported setters made their way into homes across the country as gentlemen's gundogs and favorite family dogs, most setters exhibited at dog shows in the years before World War II came from established kennels where managers, handlers and groomers were employed.

At the end of the war, new money and leisure made it possible for many middle class families to take up hobbies, and for many dog shows became a part of life. But the transformation from the large kennels to the family hobby kennel was hardly unique to the English Setter. The popularity of field trials and shows and then of breeding as a hobby was common to Gordon and Irish Setters as well.

Though the Gordon Setter is certainly less documented than the English as far as its being a unique breed in antiquity, it did benefit from the guardianship of devoted breeders, first in Scotland and then in The United States. Although no clear records exist, Setters of all kinds had been living on American soil for generations. However, in 1842 well before any of the other setter breeds have documented imports, two Black and Tan Setters were purchased by George Blunt of New York City directly from his Grace, the Duke of Gordon. Blunt family members later reported that from these two setters, Rake and Rachael—the latter going to Daniel Webster—came sufficient stock to stamp a line of quality gundogs.[22] Yet many more must have arrived on this side of the Atlantic to account for the extraordinary numbers entered at the first Westminster Dog Show in New York City in 1877. Classes were offered for more than sporting dogs and forty-five breeds were represented. Among the nine sporting breeds were English Setters with an

Gordon Setter type: Ch. Florence H. (England) 1905.

entry of 145, Irish Setters with 171 and Gordons with 79. Native and imported divisions were listed for all the setters. Obviously the Scottish Setter—or the Black and Tan Setter as it was called for many years before the adoption in the late 1800's of the name honoring the Duke had arrived as a permanent member of the pure-bred dog fancy in America. As was common in the case of the English Setters, Gordons had a moneyed following: the Belmonts, Inglees, Nivens, and later Mrs. Sherman Hoyt and the Andrews of Pittsburgh.[23] The famous wildlife artist of the early1920's and 1930's, C. Cass Hendee, was owner of the Highland Kennels (see color plate 14 by Hendee) and Percy Roberts handled Gordons.[24]

For many years in both the United States and the British Commonwealth, Gordon Setters, although represented by fine individual dogs and bitches, lacked a common type. The reasons for this become clear when we examine the developing years of the breed. According to Gilbert Leighton-Boyce[25], the Black and Tan Setter was established in England by 1726. Most writers agree that the history of this setter is impossible to document, but it is admitted by all that the English Setter and the Irish Red and Irish Red and White Setters must at one time have been contributors to the breed. In addition, as has been previously stated, these interbreedings continued into the twentieth century. The Gordon, therefore, did not benefit from the depth and breadth of a breeding base such as was common to the other setters. Yet there are interesting facts at hand. Watson gives a very helpful synopsis of the noted writers on Black and Tans:

> Stonehenge seemed to be of the opinion that the ancestors of the Gordon strain came from Ireland, but there was no need to introduce the reds to get the tan, for black and tan is one of the old setting spaniel colours. Caius before 1576 wrote regarding spaniels that 'Othersome of them be reddish and blackishe, but of that sort there be very few.' Markham in the early part of the seventeenth century said that 'black and fallow are esteemed the hardest to endure.' The Rev. Mr. Simons in 1776 wrote as follows:

> 'Whatever mixtures may have been since made, there were fifty years ago, two distinct tribes—the black-tanned and the orange or lemon and white.'

Edward Laverack was well acquainted with the Black and Tan and called it a fashionable and favorite breed. He further related that he had "gone twice to Broughty Ferry, near Dundee, for the express purpose of inspecting the kennel of that veteran sportsman, Major Douglas, a contemporary of the late Alexander, Duke of Gordon and Lords Panmure and Wemyss. The black tans I saw …were strong and powerful but…headstrong dogs."[26] The Rev. Mr. Hutchinson, known as "Sixty One," was known for his good breed of black tans, and according to Laverack the dogs were lighter and not as cumbersome as many of the others.[27] The Druid reports that in his knowledge of the breed there were kennels that had only black tans and that they were not light in frame but were good at their work. These were owned by Lord Halliburton, Major Douglas and Lord Breadalbane.[28] The Druid also states that he had been to Gordon Castle after the death of Alexander and all the dogs he found were black, white, and tan. His assumption was that the Duke had always preferred the better gundog to the dog's color and that the tri-colors were easier to see on the hill side as the darker dogs.[29] Finally, Laverack concludes that the Gordon needed some improvements which he described thus: "The coat should be silky and slightly wavy and intensely black. The tan, a deep mahogany or burnt sienna colour. (And) to render these dogs lighter, give them better heads, more endurance but keep their colour."[30] Although it is accepted that The Duke of Gordon and others used crosses with Lord Lovat's black English Setters and perhaps even used Irish Setter crosses, the most controversial subject discussed by every writer on Gordon Setters is whether there were crosses used by His Grace or others from outside of the sporting dog family. Most writers think it feasible that in order to improve the working quality of the breed, that a Scotch Collie was introduced. Only the purists of recent years have dismissed this as something close to treason. A number of accounts do suggest that the men who worked at the Castle Gordon or on neighboring estates believed it was true. That a "very clever black and tan collie bitch was acquired from a nearby farm and was used with the black tans and the black, tans and whites were mentioned by Idstone who said that he was familiar with individual dogs at the castle that were long in loin, that carried tails like a collie and that tended to run around its game as if to herd it.[31] If a collie cross was used, the early standard can be seen as a guide to eradicate the undesirable qualities while adhering to the characteristics that had been established by the breeders before the time of Gordon Castle.

Today there is a strength and consistency among Gordon Setters thanks to the dedicated breeders who for years had the patience to strive for type and to use the standard as a guide. And according to a number of judges who have seen the Gordons in Australia during the past twenty years, that is where the best of the old country and the best of America has been judiciously used to create a superb population of Gordon Setters.

Chronology of Setter Documentation

The following list is a synopsis of what has been presented by many writers as the historical background of the setters. Interpretations of the documentation vary and the original literature should be consulted for exact words and meaning.

Date	Documentation	Description
1066	The Bayoux Tapestry	Small halking dogs taken from England to Normandy
1300's	Red & White Spaniels	Spaniels established in England (white with red, white with black, white with liver)
1400's	The Devonshire Tapestry	Falconry as a sport to take birds shown with men and women in the field
1406	Gaston De Foix	Detailed description of the setter work pattern
1550	Shooting Flying	Descriptions of use of guns to take birds (Europe)
1500's	Setting Dogs	Exist in England and Ireland
1500's	Pointers	Referred to as existing in Italy, Spain and France (no clear documentation)
1563	Setter by name	Lord Warwick to brother, Robert Dudley "I will send you the best setter in France."
1576	Setter is named	Dr. Caius labels the "Setting Spaniel" as Index in Latin or Setter
1582	Setter in drawing	Hans Bols describes and shows a white setter on partridges and a hunter with crossbow. He shows spaniels as different from setters.
1634	Red Irish Setter	Exists in England (see Color Plate 3)
1600's	Setting Dogs	Frequent references from many writers
1624	Setting Dog as Gift	From Louis XIII of France to James I of England
1650's	Pointer in France	Referred to as originating in Italy and Spain (no specific documentation)

Date	Documentation	Description
1660	Shooting Flying	Descriptions of use of guns to take birds (England)
1655	Black and Tan	Markham refers to setters but no link exists between Markham and the later setters called Gordons
1714	Multi-use of Setting Dogs	Falconry, Netting and shooting were all used in England
1680-1755	Setter Type	France: Paintings by Francois Desportes and Jean Babtiste Oudry
1706-1736	Pointers in England	From area of Amsterdam and from France (No specific documentation from Spain)
1726	Black and Tan Setters	Established in England
1700's	Red and White Setter	Established in England
1770's	Irish Red Setter	Self-colored Red Setters become more popular in Ireland
1842	Gordon Setter Import	George Blunt imported Rake and Rachael from The Duke of Gordon
1874	First U.S.A. dog shows	Chicago, Mineola, NY and Memphis Pointers and Setters only[1]
1874	Irish Setters Imported	Most had direct lines from Hutchinson's Bob. (Ireland)
1874	English Setters Imported	Charles Raymond bought a brace from Laverack

1. *The AKC's World of the Pure-Bred Dog* (1983) documents these shows as the first held in the United States.

In the early writings and paintings of setters in Great Britain, Ireland, and the United States, there is a setter that is often described and seen that most inquirers of recent times as being a miss-marked English or a Welsh Springer that has gone a bit wrong. But recent explanations have established that this indeed is the "fourth setter"—The Irish Red and White Setter. Patricia Brigden in her superb text on the breed published in England in 1990 has reason to claim that this is the setter of the greatest antiquity. Twenty-five years ago Mrs. Maxwell explained that the original Irish Setters had been, in fact, predominantly white with red patches[32] and suggested that although it remains undocumented the Irish Setter could very well be the oldest of the setters. Of all the setter histories, that of the Red and White is certainly the most interesting—not only because the breed is still rare (in the United States it is still limited to competition at shows held by the American Rare Breeds Association), but because the breed, now that we know what we are looking at, is everywhere. The American Kennel Club has more paintings of Red and Whites than of Gordons. In Ireland and Great Britain there are significant collections of paintings, both private and public, that depict individuals of the breed. Many of the paintings are with people or in places that document that the breed existed and by name. Reproductions of paintings published in the United States in the form of postcards, calendars and wall hangings usually depict the Red and White in the field. And while the breed's all but exclusive affiliation with field pursuits has until recently kept it from gaining wide public familiarity, the Red and White story is not as simple as one might therefore expect.

First, it has been documented that the very earliest spaniels, from which the setter is said to have evolved, were white with red patches. These dogs were to be found in Europe and in England as early as the 1300's, and were described as white with patches of red, and white with patches of black or liver. With the distinction made in the 1500's, that setting dogs in Ireland and England were separate from the spaniels, comes the first clue to the existence of a setter that was used for birds and small game and that was red and white.[33] Not only is it known that Caius included red and white in his description of the setter, but by the early 1600's clear evidence indicates the existence in Ireland and England of setters that were both white with red and red with white.[34] The Nathaniel Bacon self portrait dated 1625 presented in the Leighton-Boyce book shows the artist with his favorite possessions, including his setting dog which is described in the literature as white with red patches. From that time on, the existence of the red and white setter can be documented in paintings, and by the 1700's there is also written confirmation of established kennels devoted to setters that were exclusively white with red or red with white. Breeders of these dogs made highly significant contributions during the mid 1700's. The Rossmore family of Rossmore Castle, County Monaghan began a separate strain of red and whites at this time, a line which was to continue for almost two hundred years. Paintings in the family collection are still in existence and trace the generations of setters that pleased the Lords of Rossmore.[35] From the beginning, setters of all colors were bred for the chief purpose of hunting, yet the Irish Red and White continued to fulfill that role even after other setter breeds were defined and preserved by the advent of dog shows. In Ireland the dog existed not only on the estates, but later as a dog of general utility in hunting small game in the harsh, rocky environments. This fourth setter became popular as a member of the family, and pictures in recent histories of Ireland show it as a common fixture in the Irish kitchen. It is probable that during the time when the breed was well known writers either subsumed it under the greater classification of Irish Setter or identified it as an English Setter. At the Rotunda Show in Dublin in 1863, Irish Setters were entered representing both coat colors. But after that period the whole-colored dog became dominant, and the Irish Red and White was again relegated to the field and the kitchen when fashion held that it was not equal to the solid mahoganies.[36] According to Brigden, "The revival of the Irish Red and White Setter begins just after the Great War and spans the period up to the present day." [37] Many contributors, first in Ireland and then in Great Britain, have literally saved the breed from extinction by finding setters that displayed or carried the red and white patterning. Because these setters were always perceived as gun dogs, the revival included careful choices of Irish Setters that came from the ranks of the field trial competitors or field strains. Notable in their contributions to the revival of the Irish Red and White Setter during the twentieth century are The Rev. Noble Houston, Canon Patrick Doherty, and—primus inter pares—Mrs. Maureen Cuddy of Knockalla fame. The Irish Red and White

Setter Society was formed in 1944, and a standard that was meant to focus on the dogs' use in the field was drawn up. As a precursor to inclusion in the Irish Kennel Club registry, documentation of pure breeding lines was written and presented by Mrs. Cuddy in 1970. In 1982 at the Swords Championship Show in Ireland (see photo in Chapter Four) there was a celebration of the success of the revival with an excellent entry of Irish Red and White Setters from Ireland and the United Kingdom. The judge was Maureen Cuddy and her critique of the entry, published in the Brigden book, represents her lifetime of experience in the breed.

In the United States, The Irish Red and White Setter Club of America was established in 1984 for the purposes of promoting the breed and working toward the AKC recognition of the breed. The club was incorporated in 1996, Mr. and Mrs. Bob Humphrey organized the newsletter, and Curtis Humphrey published a compilation of facts about the breed for the membership and for judges. The first National Specialty was held in Georgia in 1987, and the first national Hunting Test was held in 1995 in Pennsylvania. The standard presently in use is taken from the Irish Standard, but it has specific limits to prevent artificial grooming that would change the natural look of this working setter.

Today the Irish Red and White Setter is exhibited at championship shows in all countries where there are classes offered except for the United States, where the American Kennel Club is reviewing the breed for Miscellaneous Class status. The standard describes a setter that is different from all the others, setting it apart from the English Setter by proscribing flecking except on the lower legs and muzzle, and from the Irish by its more level topline (although the natural ruff of hair over the withers may make it appear that the dog is higher at the top of the shoulder) and it must be examined to see if that is true. Its only similarity to the Gordon Setter is a rounder rib cage than other setters. The head of the Red and White is unique, with a shallow-flewed muzzle and no definition of the occiput. The breed should appear "athletic", but not racy; strong and well developed, but not carrying the bone weight of the other setters. Finally, the Irish Red and White Setter has been preserved because it was the setter with "the best nose" and the greatest intensity of hunting instinct.[38] Therefore the breed today must look like its purpose—hearty, well protected by coat, swift of foot and built for endurance. It did not rise again from the shamrocks. It has been revived by the tenacity of breeders in the twentieth century, and the breed exists with some diversity of type but with a growing breeding base that will serve the future.

While the Red and White Setter of Ireland gave to its progeny the will to hunt and the stamina to endure, the breeders in the late 1700's saw fit to eliminate the ancient jacket pattern and select for the solid color dogs. White on the head, feet and chest was acceptable but the less the better. By the time the first dog shows were held one hundred years later, the setter of Ireland was a mahogany dog with only traces of white allowed by the fashion of the day.

Nonetheless, the evidence (some of it by deduction) suggests that the solid color comes much earlier and that the setters in Ireland were of two types: one from the red hunting dogs that are described in France, and the other from the more spaniel-like red and whites that are known to be common in Ireland. These two kinds of dogs at some point no doubt were interbred. But Mrs. Maxwell, puzzled that Ireland had a setter that was not of the same color or anatomical construction as the other setters, looked further for an explanation.[39] The Welsh Spaniel, certainly a dog with the classic shallow-flewed headpiece that is similar to the Irish Setter, does not have the tall upright more pointer like build of the setters known as Irish. Also, there is no direct link ever suggested between the spaniel and the Irish Setter unless the spaniel coat is taken as enough evidence and that because all setters are related if one comes from the spaniel then all must. In his 1927 *Irish Setter History* Col. Shilbred notes, "It is odd that of all the setters the Irish is the farthest removed in type from the spaniels."[40] Among the sporting breeds only the pointer is constructed like the Irish Setter, but that does not seem to fit unless the pointers from France had gotten to Ireland which, indeed, could have occurred. However, what does create a possibility is the link to the hunting hounds of France that were also similar in body and legs to the later European pointers. George Turberville, in his book *The Noble Art of Venerie or Hunting* published in 1575, describes the dogs as the hounds of the French hunting pageantry.[41] Among the various descriptions, the following is for these purposes the most important: "some had long ears and Tayles shagged like Ears of Corn...and some were a lively Redde."[42] In other words there were longhaired hunting hounds in France at that time and they were "fast, hardy, endured pain and Travayle" and they were red![43] And as W. Enos Phillips has suggested, the link by water route between France, Ireland and Scotland was a common one and it would be plausible that these red hounds had gone at least as far as Ireland. Anna Redlich in her *The Dogs of Ireland* written in 1949, cites the writings of a seventeenth century Primate of Ireland, but they shed no new light on the origins of the Irish Setter.[44] Watson attempts to link the Irish Setters to hounds, but he does so by way of the dark greyhounds of England.[45] The arch over

Irish Setter type: Triple International Champion Domnal MacGruagach. (Ireland) 1907.

the loin certainly has been part of the Irish Setter build that is common knowledge to all who know the breed. But the unique Irish color likely began in France.

The evidence of the Irish Setter antiquity, however, has only recently been available in color illustration. Color plate 3 shows a typical Irish Setter of contemporary characteristics in a painting by Anthony Van Dyck in England in 1634. In addition the Irish Setter, also in color by Sydenham Edwards in 1805 illustrates the depth of the mahogany color and the presence of the white blaze on the face (see color plate 5).

The writers of the 1800's including Laverack who tried crossing Irish Setters with his blue belton English Setters, did not create a favorable press for the glamorous breed that called Ireland its home. Laverack held that by the 1860's the breed had degenerated.[46] Other writers described the dog as headstrong, hard to break, and lacking in endurance. The modern reader might conclude that the fast growing popularity of the Red Setter and its success at field trials in England and then in the United States created a threat to other setter fanciers. The bias in reasoning on the part of writers in England in the late 1800's could also have been a question of national pride.

But once the Irish Setter had "arrived" and was accepted as an equal to any of the setters, it would never be seen as anything but a spectacular dog. The exports from Ireland and England were numerous, and kennels in the United States began to embrace not only the field pursuits but also the dog show. And it would be in the context of the dog show that the Irish Setter found its natural home. The dog was aesthetically exciting to watch with its bold manner, its rugged good looks and that shiny, silky coat of dark mahogany—the color of a newly opened chestnut.

Today the only time that Irish Setters are discussed in a negative manner is by those who have not trained the dog properly or understood its' needs. It is a busy breed and the term "rollicking" that is used in the standard describes it best. Irish Setters are the tallest of the setters and they are extroverts by nature. Their manner, however is always friendly and "willing to give anything a go." They are trustworthy with all members of the family and they are of good deportment with other dogs. The Irish is also a long-lived breed of high intelligence and the lucky family who own one will enjoy the dog for more years than most setters can give.

The goal of this chapter is certainly not to take the place of the extraordinary depth of information that is vital to today's fancier and available in the individual breed textbooks. This effort has instead focused on old writings and illustrations that offer documentation and that inspire new inquiries. The goal has also been to describe the breeds as they were long ago in such a way as to help the modern fancier understand the words and intent of the standards that exist today. Finally, with a better understanding and respect for the past, the breeders of today will be able to rise to the challenge of being the future guardians of the diverse "tribes" of setters.

Endnotes

1   *A Survey of Early Setters* by Gilbert Leighton-Boyce (1985).

2   *The Truth About Sporting Dogs* by C. Bede Maxwell (1972).

3   *All Setters* by Freeman Lloyd (1931). Also in *The Complete English Setter* by Davis Tuck (1951).

4   Leighton-Boyce (1985).

5   Ibid.

6   *The True Pointer and His Ancient Heritage* by W. Enos Phillips (1970).

7   *A History and Description of Modern Dogs of Great Britain and Ireland* by Rawdon Lee (1893).

8   Vero Shaw *The Illustrated Book of the Dog* (1890).

9   Phillips (1970).

10 *Livre de Chase* by Gaston DeFoix English translation (1406-1413), modern translation (1909). In Maxwell (1972).

11 Phillips (1970).

12 Ibid.

13 Oudry depicts a setter from a royal kennel with the tail shaved in the fashion of the day.

14 In Maxwell (1972) as well as original literature.

15 Setters were used in Europe, Great Britain and Ireland to hunt both fur and feathers.

16 *The Dog Book* by James Watson (1909).

17 *The Setters* by Edward Laverack (1872).

18 Ibid.

19 Ibid.

20 Ibid.

21 The inter-breeding between the setters continued well into the early years of the twentieth century. Some of these crosses were for better field workers and some were honest errors of kennel management.

22 Lloyd (1931).

23 *Popular Dogs* (1961).

24 *The Complete Gordon Setter* by Jean Look (1984).

25   Leighton-Boyce (1985).

26   Laverack (1872).

27   Ibid.

28   Watson (1909).

29   Laverack (1872).

30   Ibid.

31   Watson (1909).

32   Maxwell (1972).

33   Leighton-Boyce (1985).

34   Ibid.

35   Brigden (1990).

36   *The Irish World: The Art and Culture of the Irish People* published by Harrison House/Abrams, Inc. New York. 1986 and also in: Watson (1909).

37   Brigden (1990).

38   Watson (1909).

39   Maxwell (1972).

40   Ibid. (In Maxwell).

41   Ibid.

42   Ibid.

43   Ibid.

44   Ibid.

45   Watson (1909).

46   Laverack (1872).

2 | The English Setter

$\mathscr{T}$he French knew it as a Coucher; Johannes Caius wrote of it in Latin as Index, (translation: setter); later writers referred to it as an improved spaniel; and more recently in the up-country areas of New England the old Yankees called the English Setter, "them partridge dogs"—of course pronouncing it "pat-rige." This setter with the coat of many colors that Rawdon Lee[1] describes as, "gaudily blue and white or orange and white, has been written about and documented for centuries. Its hunting ability and genial manner made it popular with the nobility, the landed gentry, and the private citizen. Today we know it to be a competent gundog especially for hunters on foot. And although this purpose has always been the breed's guiding influence, the English Setter has been preserved in correct type by the dog show fanciers who have adhered to the breed standard. While the first standard was put forth by Edward Laverack in 1872, the words and meaning have changed very little through the various editions over the years. In other words, a modern judge or breeder could be informed by the Laverack standard as well as the standards of today. This may well be the explanation for the superb quality and consistency of type of the present day dogs. The knowledgeable guardians of the breed held this to be true: "the standard sets the model or paradigm for what the English Setter must look like; we breed to the standard and never change the standard to describe the dog that we have created through whim, fashion, or anomaly.[2]

The purpose of this chapter is to explain what the English Setter must look like when it conforms to the standard. In

Ideal Female English Setter.[i]

order to do that it is necessary to first explain and dismiss the labels that have been inappropriately fixed in breed lore for one hundred and thirty years. Then temperament, conformation and the dog in motion will be discussed.

False Labels: Laverack and Llewellin

In 1825 Edward Laverack obtained from the Rev. A. Harrison two line-bred English Setters, Ponto and Old Moll, from which he developed for the next fifty years a line that would go down in dog history as the basis for the modern English Setter. He hunted his dogs, and when field trials and dog shows began he was the most successful breeder known at that time. In approximately 1865 R. LL. Purcell Llewellin purchased the finest show stock available from Laverack and commenced a breeding program of his own. Stonehenge and other writers who were contemporaries of Laverack referred to the product of the line as Dan-Laveracks because they came from either Laverack bitches or Laverack dogs that were bred to Sir Corbet's and Mr. Statter's strain, among which were Dan and his sisters.[3] The dogs used for the cross were "somewhat coarse, withal powerful workmanlike dogs"[4] but brought the

A family affair.[ii]

new blood so needed to sustain all that Laverack had worked for. Llewellin was imminently successful with his dogs both in the show ring and in the field competitions. His goal was to establish a line that had beauty, bird sense and vigor.

Thus, both men made significant contributions to the breed: while one established the breeding base, the other took it forward and strengthened it. As was previously presented in chapter one, the strains of many breeds and particularly of English Setters were commonly identified in the dog press by the name of the owner rather than by a kennel name as is today's practice. For Laverack and Llewellin there was no exception. But it must be said that neither man ever suggested nor expected that the individual lines, though so closely related, would carry their names into the future. Nor is it correct that Laverack bred for show and Llewellin bred for field. In fact, Llewellin continued to purchase dogs from Laverack because he believed that the dogs must be true setters in type in order to be good workers. According to the show catalogues in England, the English Setters of Llewellin were top winners for many years and were reported as such by Idstone, Stonehenge, Lee, Lloyd, Watson and others. Most of these writers

1836 Engraved by T. Sutherland, London. From the collection of Robert and Marsha Brown. iii

also suggest that the names of the two men who were indeed friends, were used in advertisements by others to promote the sale of dogs for export.[5] Watson suggested that the names really began being used in the United States as a stereotype for show vs. field type. And in the late 1800's in England and America that assertion simply was not accurate. In fact, the definition usually applied to the Llewellin dogs was any English Setter of the line from the Dan-Laverack crosses. By the twentieth century, while Llewellin continued to use show stock and Laverack progeny at that, he had by the reports of others also used Gordons, Irish, and other weldings to further improve his line.[6] According to Mrs. Maxwell, these later infusions created the likes of Rodrigo and the legendary Count Noble. In 1915 after the last of the straight-bred Llewellins, La Resita, won the National Field Trial Title in the United States, the shape and form of the field trial dogs began to change. What had been called in a pejorative manner "the Llewellin fault," the high tail carriage which was the antithesis of what Llewellin bred, began to become the accepted style by American sportsmen.[7] The setters from that time on were American made field setters with vague or no ties to the talented breeder from England. Therefore, the use of these terms today are but polarizing labels that show little regard for what these men really bred, showed and trialed.

English Setter puppies.[iv]

Gentlemen by nature.
Melbourne, Australia,
1982.[v]

Temperament

Although the English Setter has many other claims to fame, the characteristic that has always guaranteed its future in homes around the world is temperament. The breed is easy to train, lives to please, is dignified when necessary, and is ready to romp and run when the occasion presents itself. They can even be down right silly especially when playing in the snow, rolling in fall leaves, or playing on a beach.

Above all the English is patient. In fact, the responsible parent must be vigilant in supervising the dog and the young child because too often the dog will put up with much more than should ever be expected. However, like any setter, a puppy can be tedious and the age of a dog that is equivalent to human teen years can be challenging for the most experienced dog owner. The reward is the even-tempered, loyal, and affectionate mature setter that is trustworthy and that thrives in every type of family. While the English Setter is renowned for its demeanor, it can be overly sensitive to new experiences and environments if it is not socialized at a young age. Training must be appropriate to the breed, because these setters do not react well to harsh methods or physical discomfort. And without proper management of diet and exercise, some can become lazy and content to lounge into old age and obesity.

English Setter guarding the Columbia River.[vi]

Belles and the baby.[vii]

English Setter as companions.[viii]

Photo by Callea.

Photo courtesy of the Howe Family Collection. [ix]

Photo permission by Providence Journal.

Conformation

The standard describes a dog that is meant to be useful as well as beautiful. Therefore, the dog must be strong, energetic, and willing to participate in whatever activity is planned. The English Setter has been aptly described by John Nielsen as the moderate setter and the English Setter Association of America instructs in the official standard, "above all, extremes of anything distort type." These two concepts must be guides to understanding the breed and what it should look like. It is to be moderate in size and substance, moderate in spirit, and moderate in coat. The symmetry of the whole, not the exaggeration of parts, is the essence of the dog. In fact the attempt to draw attention to the anomalies of individual parts serves to destroy the parts which are to be in harmony. The outline or **silhouette** of the English Setter is clear: level and parallel planes to the head with a defined stop, arched brow, and clear evidence of the occipital protuberance; a long well muscled neck, a body that is slightly longer than it is tall at the withers, a level topline, deeply angled front and rear running gear, and a level tail position. The legs must be strong and well boned. The forechest is to be obvious to sight, well developed to touch

John Ward Brady and Jeannette Brady with their Frenchtown English Setters.

Ideal English Setter Male.[x]

Ideal English Setter Bitch.[xi]

Silhouette of the English Setter

English Setter

*The English Setter is level in topline and is slightly longer than it is tall. The head is **moderate** in size with less depth of skull and muzzle than the Gordon Setter and more depth of skull and muzzle than the Irish Setter. The planes of the head are parallel. The head shown above is correct but also correct is more depth of flew when it is in proportion with the skull and the substance of the whole dog. Balance of the front assembly with the rear assembly is key to correct structure. English Setters should have a well developed forechest or prosternum. Bone size is moderate and feet are well arched. The tail should be an extension of the level topline and should be presented and carried at the level of the back and not above. (Exact wording of the standards is in the appendix).*

and the feet are well arched, functional and with tough, protective pads. While the silhouette is important to commit to memory, so too are the unique characteristics of the breed.

W. Enos Phillips and C. Bede Maxwell concurred that the essence of any sporting breed can be seen in the head and the tail. That is particularly true of the English Setter.

John James Audubon, the naturalist and writer, said of the face and head of this setter, (it) "appears to have a great sense of sagacity."[8] While this term has been used elsewhere to describe the breed, it is not defined anywhere. Does it mean the English Setter is wise, insightful, keenly perceptive? Or does it mean that the dog has a keen sense of smell? In any event, the elegance of the head and face is created by the deep drop in fore-face where a smooth blend between the skull and muzzle denotes a very slight difference between the greater width of the skull and less width of the muzzle. The eyes are dark, rather large, and are set in an almond shaped rim that shows no laxity or haw. The nose is fully pigmented and of a color appropriate to the coat. It is large and moist with open nostrils. Note: English Setters that have brown, liver or dark tan noses can develop a "snow nose" that appears very light during the winter season. The flat, clean lines under the eyes, at the sides of the temple, and at the cheeks are called chiseling and must be present in the correct head. The ears are to be set low and well back so as not to intrude on the face or expression. The sum total of the details of the head and face must present a look of quiet confidence, intelligence and good manners. Individual markings on the head such as a patch or tear drop or a high ear marking that rounds up onto the skull can enhance the beauty of a specific dog. The tail of the English Setter is to be level with the back line and is often shaped with a tendency toward what in the Pointer is described as a "pump handle." Though not required, this is a characteristic that only in rare instances occurs in the other setters, and is discussed in old writings as the anomaly that prevented a high tail carriage.

Best in Show English Setter, 1968. Photos by Gilbert.[xii]

A top winner in the 1980's.[xiii]

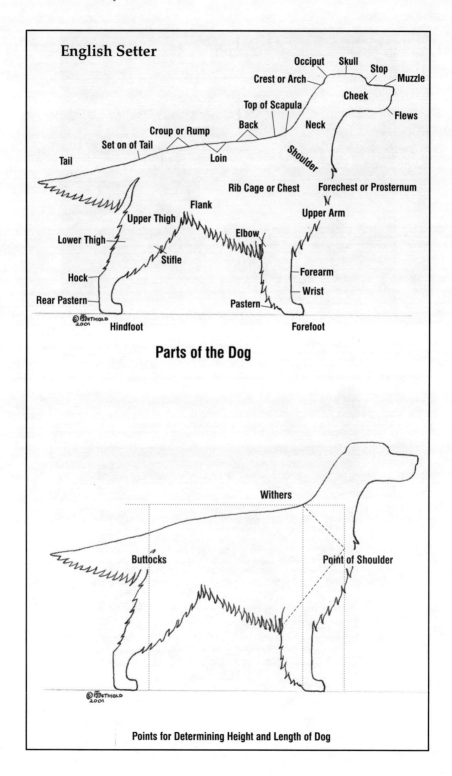

English Setter

Occiput · Skull · Stop
Crest or Arch · Muzzle
Top of Scapula · Cheek
Back · Neck · Flews
Croup or Rump · Shoulder
Set on of Tail · Loin
Tail

Rib Cage or Chest · Forechest or Prosternum
Flank · Upper Arm
Upper Thigh
Lower Thigh · Elbow
Stifle
Hock · Forearm
Rear Pastern · Wrist
Pastern
Hindfoot · Forefoot

Parts of the Dog

Withers
Buttocks · Point of Shoulder

Points for Determining Height and Length of Dog

A family of English Setters at the Detroit Kennel Club, 1956.[xiv]
Courtesy of Lishinski.

Best in Show English Setter. Chicago, 1958. [xv] Photo by William Brown.

English Setter Head Study: Female

English Setter Head Study: Male

Correct angles of the shoulder allow the setter to drop its body with ease.

While the balance of angulation between the front assembly and the rear assembly is key to the quality of all the setters, the English Setter is built correctly with greater flexibility of the shoulder, upper arm and elbow. This allows this setting dog to lower or drop its well developed rib cage to the greatest depth between the shoulder blades when "frozen" in the ancient position of the coucher. The topline of the dog in this position is strikingly beautiful with the points of the top of the scapula

1999 English Setter on Point.

Photo by Gilbert.[xvi]

Ch. Rip of Blue Bar owned by C. N. Myers.

Balance is beautiful.[xvii]

Australia's top-producing English Setter to date. (1982) Ch. Whernside Aquarius. Owned by Millie and Alex Price, Melbourne.

Puppies

Warren Brewbaker with Chandelle puppies.

Debbie Stotyn. Canada, 1990.

clearly in evidence and pointing aft, the point of the shoulder way forward, and the elbow now at the widest part of the rib cage and rotating slightly outward to allow for the slight convergence of the legs and feet below. Only the correctly built dog can do this well. Therefore, in a free standing position the back must be level and strong, blending into a well muscled loin that gives only a hint of an arch above. The hindquarters must be sufficiently well angled to balance the front, but must not be exaggerated with an overly long lower thigh. The hock is short and must be perpendicular to the ground when the dog is standing free or in a posed position. The above description of the flexibility of the front running gear is **not** intended to suggest that the elbows of the English Setter are forgivably loose. Rather it is to explain that the ancient "set to game position" is a criterion for anatomical excellence, and that the English Setter is particularly able to use its shoulders, arms and elbows in alternative ways to effect such a position.

The Dog in Motion

Laverack explains that the English Setter is to be "short above and long underneath"[9] He explains that the dog with a rather short, strong back and a short, well made loin will be able to stretch itself out in the gallop creating an underline (from the depth of the chest or brisket to the flank) that is far longer than the top. The English Setter at the gallop is not what is evaluated in the show ring, but the dog's need to gallop when at work should be taken into consideration. The trotting speed is the mode of examination, and at the trot the English Setter is to be a harmony of all parts while demonstrating that it possesses the necessary anatomy for endurance galloping. First, the dog that is balanced, even without the optimum angulation front and rear, will move with more efficiency and will have more wherewithal than the dog that is straight on one end and angled at the other.

The dog that is deeply angled and in balance will perform the trot or the gallop with less effort and less stress on all body parts and will cover more ground. The standard of the setter describes a functional animal. The level topline is part of that

English Setter at a gallop.[xviii]

Extension.

Single track at the gallop.

English Setters in Motion

Angulation and balance allows maximum reach and extension.

Made to move. This English Setter bitch is well-angulated and perfectly balanced. Note: the photograph shows a direct profile.[xix]

Making the right moves at Westminster. A classic photo of correct English Setter motion.[xx] *Photo by Glambrock.*

function. A nineteenth century writer told of setters in Wales that could carry lanterns on their backs to provide light to hunt by. While surely a fanciful exaggeration, this vividly makes the point that the English Setter must be steady. The twentieth century version of that image involves the setter carrying a teacup (with or without tea?) on its back, with the same point intended. Underneath that back and loin must be the anatomical necessities including muscles, tendons, and ligaments all of which are in healthy condition. The English Setter moves with head aloft but at an angle so that the head is inclined forward of the body. The stride of the front foot reaches to a point that is as far forward as the muzzle of the dog but the height of the foot should be only equal to the height of the wrist. The rear legs should reach forward to a point at the middle of the body and should extend under the mid point of the tail, preferably showing the pads of the rear feet. There should be no twist of the body in forward motion. This breed must move with a pleasant spirit—a willing disposition—but it should not move with the speed and the rollicking abandon of the Irish Setter. Also characteristic of the English Setter is the tail that is to flag or lash from side to side at the level of the back in a coordinated rhythm with the speed and action of the dog. This is the English Setter in pose and in motion. It is a dog built for the hunter on foot and it remains in that occupation today. And when it demonstrates its correct form in the show ring, it is a vision of symmetry and elegance. A quote from the English Setter fanciers from Australia says it all: **"On the eighth day he created setters and on the ninth day he put spots on the good ones."**

English Setter Pedigrees

The study and understanding of pedigrees is key to the establishment of a quality line of dogs. Pedigrees also tell interesting stories and can be used as a paradigm or model for the future. For example, Rummey Stagboro was a complete outcross—the result of a sire imported from Sweden and a dam of native stock. While his son, Ch. Sturdy Max was line bed—his grandam on both sides was the famous Selkirk Snooksie.

In more recent times there have been outcrosses that were highly successful in producing show winners and breeding stock. For a line to endure, however, line breeding must follow the pattern of outcrosses. Two of many examples are Ch. Guy's N Dolls Shalimar Duke, a dog that had long established his prepotency on the west coast bred to Ch. Clariho Pell of Stone Gables. The get provided the east coast lines with new vigor when used in successive linebreedings. A second example is that of Ch. Guyline's Lady Chatterley, CDX, a second generation from Guy's N Dolls, bred to Ch. Sir Kip of Manitou, a top producing dog in the east at that time.

Of further interest is the fact that in many of today's pedigrees the results of the above outcrosses have converged. The pedigree of Ch. Gold Rush Gold Miner Blues is a very close linebred example.

Double Great Grandson of Rummey Stagboro, International Ch. Rock Falls Colonel. Photo by Shafer.

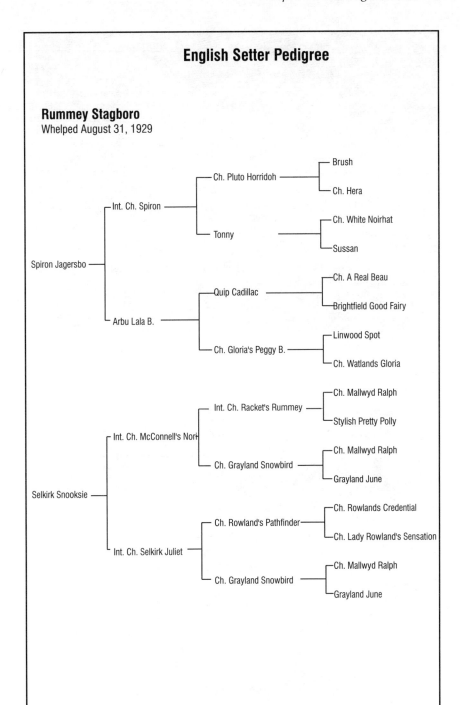

English Setter Pedigree

Rummey Stagboro
Whelped August 31, 1929

- Spiron Jagersbo
  - Int. Ch. Spiron
    - Ch. Pluto Horridoh
      - Brush
      - Ch. Hera
    - Tonny
      - Ch. White Noirhat
      - Sussan
  - Arbu Lala B.
    - Quip Cadillac
      - Ch. A Real Beau
      - Brightfield Good Fairy
    - Ch. Gloria's Peggy B.
      - Linwood Spot
      - Ch. Watlands Gloria
- Selkirk Snooksie
  - Int. Ch. McConnell's Norh
    - Int. Ch. Racket's Rummey
      - Ch. Mallwyd Ralph
      - Stylish Pretty Polly
    - Ch. Grayland Snowbird
      - Ch. Mallwyd Ralph
      - Grayland June
  - Int. Ch. Selkirk Juliet
    - Ch. Rowland's Pathfinder
      - Ch. Rowlands Credential
      - Ch. Lady Rowland's Sensation
    - Ch. Grayland Snowbird
      - Ch. Mallwyd Ralph
      - Grayland June

Ch. Sturdy Max. Photo by Tauskey.

Three month old Rock Falls Racket with William Holt.
Litter brother to Colonel.

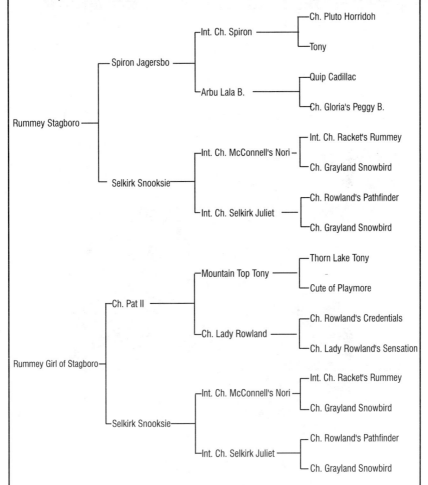

English Setter Pedigree

Ch. Sturdy Max
Whelped October 12, 1932

Outcross: *the mating of unrelated individuals*

Inbreeding: *a type of breeding program employed to obtain improvements and/or "fix" desirable physical and/or mental attributes through the mating of closely related stock such as sister/brother, father/daughter, etc.*

Linebreeding: *The concentration of characteristics of an individual or strain with an attempt to keep inbreeding at a minimum. The mating of two dogs related by direct descent.*

Endnotes

1   *Modern Dogs* by Rawdon Lee (1893).

2   Comdr. Thomas W. Hall delivered this in a speech in February 1963 at the Dog Fanciers Luncheon Club in N.Y. City.

3   Rawdan Lee (1893).

4   Ibid.

5   *The Dog Book* James Watson (1909).

6   Ibid.

7   *The Truth About Sporting Dogs* by C. Bede Maxwell (1972).

8   *The Setters* by Freeman Lloyd (1931).

9   *The Setter* by Laverack (1872).

Photo with permission of the Providence Journal.[xxi]

Photo Endnotes

i.   Ch. Frenchtown Calico Flower.

ii.   Ch. Flecka Feathers of Blue Bar, 1950.

iii.   This engraving was a gift to Comdr. Thomas W. Hall from his life-long friend and hunting partner, Walton Smith. The author inherited it from her father.

iv.   Cymbria's 'A' litter. Owned by John and Jackie Kessler.

v.   Left to Right: Ch. Engsett Empery and Ch. Whernside Endeavour. Owned by Joan and Karen Kristof.

vi   Stone Gables Out West Orator. Owned by the Edingers. 1992.

vii.   Alexander Avila and his friend.

viii.   Jack Johnson with his English Setter Can., Mex., & Am. Ch. Jolly Rector of Stone Gables, CD.

ix.   Holly Howe with Ch. Clariho Checkmate of Crit-du.

x.   Ch. Silvermine Wagabond. Owned by Silvermine Kennels.

xi.   Aust. and NZ Ch. Engsett Extra Promise. (Imp. UK)

Photo courtesy of the Osterling Family Collection.

xii.   Am., Can., Brm., Ch. Sir Kip of Manitou. Handled by William Trainor for Beth and Stan Silverman.

xiii. Ch. English Accent of Valley Run with owner Rachael Van Buren.

xiv.   Left to Right: The champions from Hidden Lane: Ray O'Connell with Darby of Cary Lane, Chuck Herendeen with Ben-Dar's Replica, Horace Hollands with Ludar of Blue Bar, Gerry Hollands with Ben-Dar's Advance Notice, Carol Hollands with Ben-Dar's Winning Stride, Marge O'Connell with Ben-Dar's Carbon Copy and Melinda Hollands with Ben-Dar's Sweet Sue.

xv.   Ch. Ben-Dar's Winning Stride with owner Marge O'Connell of Hidden Lane Kennels and Hayden Martin.

xvi   Ch. Skidby Bo'Sun of Stone Gables, 1965. Owned by the author.

xvii. Australian Ch. Kinsett Kracker Jack. Owned by Mr. & Mrs. J. B. King. 1982.

xviii. Fieldplay's Sarah of Cymbria CGC.

xix.   Ch. Goodtime's Silk Teddy, the top-winning English Setter to date. Owned by Angie and Craig Sparkes.

xx.   Am., Can., Ch. Set'r Ridge's Solid Gold. Owned by Melissa Newman.

xxi.   Left to Right: Ch. Skidby Bo'Sun of Stone Gables and Ch. Prince of Deerfield.

3 | The Gordon Setter

by Dawn Ferguson

*W*hat is the ideal Gordon? How can this question be answered when there are different standards for the breed around the world, different breeding lines which are no longer traceable to the breed's first emergence in Scotland, and different interpretations by a wide variation of judges—each coming from his or her unique experiences and study methods? And when we add the beliefs, biases, and sometimes emotional decision making of those most responsible for the existence of Gordon Setters today—the breeders themselves—the feat of establishing a workable criterion seems all but impossible. This article nonetheless attempts to demonstrate that describing the appearance, performance, and personality of the Gordon Setter is indeed possible across international boundaries. Some interesting evidence exists to support this thesis. First, during the past twenty years an increase in the number of dogs imported and exported has all but eliminated the once isolated bloodlines favored by some breeders. Second, and more important, both domestic and international judges have shown over and over again that they agree on the excellent dogs and tend to agree even on the good dogs by their placements in exhibitions. Yet before Gordon Setter similarity and consistency is addressed, it is necessary to look briefly at the past.

Initially, the sole purpose of the breed was for sport and hunting. And as these setters continued to be bred for that purpose in Scotland, a rudimentary type began to emerge, a class of dogs defined by purpose and differentiated (at least publicly)

Photo by W. Brown. [i]

from the other setters. Yet in the writings of those who had first hand knowledge of the early kennels, we find that certainly other setters and even other types of dogs were part of the admixture. In the latter part of the nineteenth century, when the sport of exhibiting dogs at shows began, a set of criteria was drawn up and a standard for the breed was established, first in America and then in England. Because the Gordon's history is a mixed one with dogs being exported to America, New Zealand, Australia and the European countries, a standard became an essential blueprint for the definition and development of the breed. Yet there were different standards. In America, although the Gordon was intended for the same purpose as in its country of origin, the first enthusiasts considered the terrain sufficiently different from that of Scotland that they designed a standard which they regarded suitable for the dog's best performance in the fields of America. And despite their differences both standards proved efficient and physiologically sound for hunting purposes.

Yet even with standards in place additional complexities occurred. Gordon Setters spread to many corners of the globe, and wherever the breed became isolated for any period of

Dawn Ferguson with her top-winning Gordon Setter Bitch.

time, small variations gradually appeared. Besides, owners and breeders were influenced by their local environments and felt comfortable and satisfied with the dogs they were used to seeing. Leonardo DaVinci said it best: "Knowledge of a thing engenders love of it." We know that even today we can identify trends in a breeding line, similarities in geographical areas, and commonalities within countries.

Even if every breeder faithfully followed the standards, unexpected variations would appear—some acceptable and some not. The reasons for this are numerous; and when considering that selections made in the past served such different purposes as field, show, and obedience, not to mention variations in grooming, preferences for style, size, temperament, color, body conformation and even methods of exhibiting and presentation, it is surprising that there remains a significant degree of consistency around the world. And that brings us back to the question: What is the ideal Gordon Setter? The description will be presented in four parts: temperament, conformation, motion, and evaluation.

Temperament

Every owner in every home, in a show, at a trial, in every country, will probably declare that his or her Gordon is the best; for love is in the eyes of the beholder, and the Gordon is a dog that engenders that love. It is characteristic of this breed to become a close family member with the stability and flexibility of temperament to be gentle and patient with the toddler, trustworthy with growing children, fun loving with the teen, an intelligent working companion with men and women, and a considerate companion with the aging. Yet the Gordon is expected to function successfully in other situations. In the show ring the breed can be aloof with strangers, and therefore early socialization outside the home and at puppy matches is important. In show competition the dog must exhibit not only confidence and happy acceptance in a standing examination, but an alert and "willing to join in the game" attitude when in motion. To excel in field pursuits, the Gordon, like the other setters, is best introduced to his ancient instincts early in life while tasks, work, and rules are fun. Yet the breed is known for willingness and eagerness to work hard at any age as well as its courage and ability to stick to the task to please the hunter.

Gordon Setter as a Companion

Ch. Halenfred Scorched Gold. Providence County Kennel Club, 1952. Photo with permission from The Providence Journal.

Photo by Fitzgerald.

Harold Sydney handling Ch. Halenfred Scorched Gold to best of breed at GSCA Specialty under Percy Roberts, 1956. Photo by Brown.

Conformation

The outline or silhouette of the Gordon Setter should evidence both elegance and substance. The head must be noble with contours well defined—larger than the other setters yet in proportion with the whole dog. The neck, body and running gear are those of a well muscled, all day hunter showing strength and development of bone. The angulation of the front must place the legs well under the dog and the angulation of the rear must provide the necessary balance for the dog in motion. The back is rather short so that the dog appears well up on leg and the tail is a level extension of the level topline. Balance of form is the key to a proper Gordon. Obtrusive excesses lead to off-type specimens.

The relationship between the skull and muzzle is described as brick on brick but the Gordon "brick" is of more depth than that of the Irish Setter. The head is chiseled, of moderate size, with defined stop, and lean under the eyes. The foreface, viewed from above and side, should have a square appearance and the bridge of the nose must be straight—neither Roman nor dished. The length of the muzzle is equal to the length of the skull and the planes of each should be parallel. The skull

A quality bitch.[ii] Photo by Gilbert.

should be slightly rounded—arched from ear to ear and around the rear of the skull—unlike the English or the Irish head contours. The rims of the eyes are oval with tight lids and neither bulging or sunken. Loose rims and incorrect placement of the eye are detrimental to the health, safety, and vision of a gun dog. The eyes are dark brown, the dark of the eyeball should fill the eye opening, and the haw must not be obvious. The nose is large and black with wide, open nostrils. Complete dentition, essential to a healthy dog, includes six large, even, regular incisors above and below meeting in a scissor bite, although in the United States a pincer or level bite is permissible. Premolars are required to be present and are particularly essential to judges from European and South American countries.

Ears are low set on the skull, formed from thin leather, and long enough to reach the end of the muzzle.

The characteristic color and markings on the head give the Gordon its unique expression. First, the color is a rich tan, mahogany, or deep chestnut clearly divided from the black. Eyebrows are no bigger than three-quarters of an inch, and cheek color must not go over the nose. Also the tan extends under the jaw and down the throat. There is usually a thumb

Jean Look with Ch. Sangerfield Tracy, 1958. Photo courtesy of John Lawreck.

spot of tan under the ears, and the inside of the ears may hold tan as well (see the standard in the appendix for complete wording).

The head is clean-lined and free from unnecessary weight such as excess flew, heavy dewlap, thick ear flaps, and loose skin folds. The Gordon expression is intelligent, and both the male and female head exhibit substance and depth and are in proportion to the size of the body. Males should not be coarse nor females overly refined. Either extreme leads to off-type.

The neck is heavily muscled, arched and capable of supporting the head at a 10:30 angle; when the dog is moving at a fast speed, however, the neck inclines forward and lower. The strength and efficiency of the neck is essential to the front assembly and to the practical matter of carrying game. Of critical importance is the neck's junction with the shoulders. The neck must fit into the shoulder in a smooth line without a sharp break, angle, or wrinkle due to an upright shoulder placement. However, a deviation in this area may be acceptable if it is the result of heavy muscling in a mature dog or in a dog that has been doing heavy work.

Courtesy of the Chevalier Collection.[iii]

Harold Sydney handling Ch. Halenfred Bright Deil to Best of Breed under Virgil Johnson at the Gordon Setter Speciality, Westchester, 1954.

Ch. Wee Jock Adair, CD age 7. Sire of 33 champions. Photo by Gilbert.

Ch. Lock Adair Peer of Sutherland.

Ch. Afternod Cutty Sark. 1965. Photo by Shafer.

Challenge Dog and Bitch Melbourne, Australia, 1982.

Head Study

Head Study

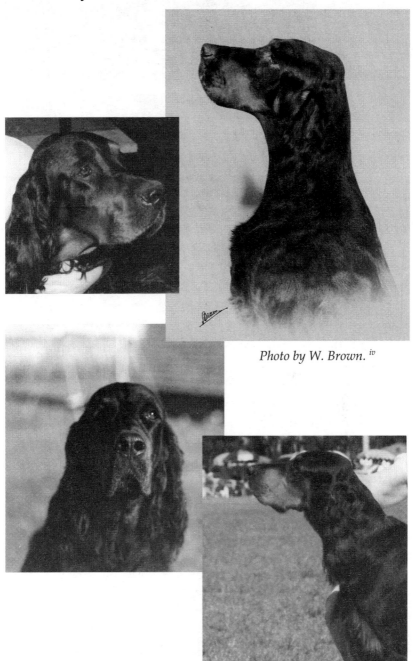

Photo by W. Brown. [iv]

Ideal Gordon Setter Male.

The body consists of an oval thoracic section (see diagram). In length the oval extends from the forechest or prosternum to the last rib, up to but not including the loin. In depth it reaches from the withers (the top of scapula) to the keel or breastbone, with the lowest point of the thoracic section on a line with the elbow. Viewed from above, the Gordon body displays ample width or spring of rib. As in all the setters, however, the ribs must be angled back from the vertebrae as they spring outward in order to enable lung distension during strenuous work. The Gordon will definitely have more width than the other setter breeds, but it must not be out of proportion or such as to make the dog appear heavy, cumbersome, or coarse. The well-built hunter should have a fairly short back that is level and strong with the back being measured from behind the withers to the attachment of the last rib. In other words, the back is but one part of the length of the dog. The loin area must be of sufficient length for the dog to make turns at speed with stability. The loin area must also be extremely well muscled to facilitate the redistribution of weight during the gallop.

The rear assembly is strong with the pelvis tending toward the horizontal and of good length to accommodate necessary muscle attachments. The tilt of the pelvis determines topline, the reach, and extension of the rear running gear. Two terms are used to discuss this area: pelvis and croup. While the pelvis identifies the skeletal formation, the croup identifies the musculature just above and around the set on of the tail and above the lower pelvis. On a Gordon Setter the croup should be fairly level. The tail should be set on so that it appears to be a smooth extension of the topline and should not rise above the level of the back nor measure longer than to the hock joint. The topline of the Gordon Setter is a significant characteristic of the breed and must not be misunderstood by breeder or judge. The correctly made Gordon has a level topline; a deficiency in this matter indicates a fault of nature or of the handler or both.

The running gear of the Gordon Setter is designed to carry this rugged hunter over rough terrain at a gallop or at a fast trot. Therefore, the limbs are to be strong with well-developed bone that is oval in shape and that appears flat on the sides. The bone mass is larger than the other setters. The front legs are vertical for optimum support of the body and are placed

Ideal Gordon Setter Female.

Gordon Setter Silhouette

© PJDETMOLD
2001

Gordon Setter

The Gordon Setter is slightly sloping in topline with a level, short back (the back is measured from behind the withers to the beginning of the loin) and is described in the United States as more square than the other setters when measured from the point of the shoulder to the rear of the back leg. Because of the furnishings of the Gordon it will appear slightly longer than it is tall. The Gordon is slightly taller than the English Setter but not as tall as the Irish Setter. The characteristic unique to the Gordon is its degree of substance in bone and body development—that is more than the other setters but must never look cumbersome or coarse. The head, in skull and muzzle, is deeper (longer from the top of the skull to the bottom of the jaw line and longer from the top of the muzzle to the bottom line of the muzzle. The top of the skull because of its greater width than the other setters, may appear in profile as very slightly rounded but the planes of the head are parallel. The Gordon has a well developed forechest or prosternum, must appear up on leg to the extent that the height is in proportion with the overall length, and must be in correct balance between the forequarters and the rearquarters. Gordons that are exaggerated in any part that sets them out of balance are not correct. The feet, well arched, are larger and rounder than the other setters. The tail is presented as an extension of the topline and is to be carried level with the topline. (Exact wording of the standards is in the appendix)

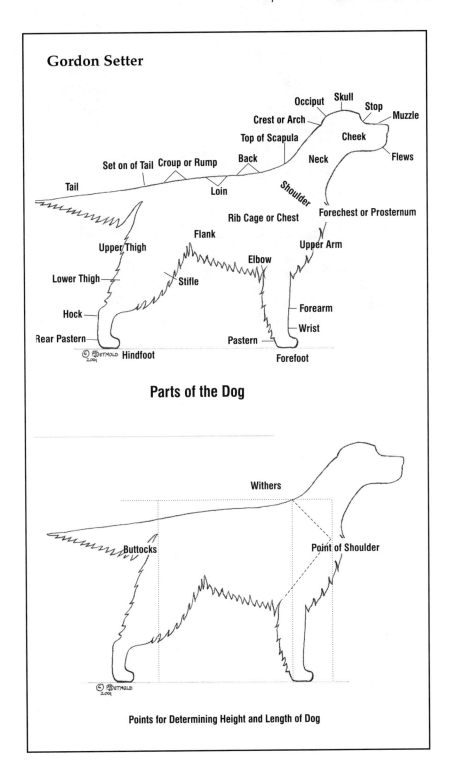

Parts of the Dog

Points for Determining Height and Length of Dog

Photo by Bergman.[v]

well under the dog (see diagram). This requires that the angle created by the junction of the shoulder blade and upper arm approaches that of a right angle. The rear limbs must be equally well developed with similar bone size and shape and obvious muscling. The upper and lower thighs must meet at a well bent stifle joint, supported by a hock that must be perpendicular to the ground. The feet should be round according to the AKC standard. In other countries feet are described as oval—designed for climbing and jumping on rougher ground. In all standards the feet should be well arched and proportionally larger than those of the other setters. Pasterns should be round to the touch and when viewed from the front should be straight. When viewed from the side the pasterns should be slightly sloping so that they may function as shock absorbers. **Of Vital Importance Is The Balance Between The Angles Of The Front And The Angles Of The Rear.** Exaggerated length of the lower thigh will not balance with the front assembly and will result in an incorrect topline, a lack of stability and support for the body, and a need to compensate in movement for the structural fault.

Photo by Olsen. 1982.[vi]

Photo by Tatham.[vii]

Gordon Setter in Germany. Photo courtesy of Muriel Clement.

The Dog in Motion

A Gordon Setter with correct skeletal build and balance does not always perform perfectly either in the ring or in the field. Muscles, tendons, ligaments, physical conditioning, and in no small measure temperament and attitude play important roles in the way the dog moves. When moving at a brisk trot, the Gordon should carry a level top line. The correct angles of the front and rear, the level croup and the length of leg in correct proportion to the length of the body allow the dog to reach forward as well as extend behind. Bouncing, jerking, or pounding motions are counter productive for an all-day hunter. The dog must cover ground in an effortless manner and the handler must allow the dog to "have its head" so that from the first front reach the dog will achieve that necessary level topline and an elevation of the front foot that is no higher than the height of the pastern. The neck should be naturally inclined forward. From the front view the Gordon should move with legs and feet that reach forward and are in a straight line of support from the elbow to the pastern to the ground. Viewed from the front a well-developed chest provides the necessary width so that the elbows lie close to the sides of the chest and are free from interference with the rib cage. From the rear, the dog should be as wide across the pelvis as at the shoulder. This width should extend down the length of the rear limbs to the foot. Although many handlers set the rear feet wider apart for a variety of reasons, and the Gordon may place its own feet wider for a quick start, the width of the dog in motion begins with legs parallel. Like the other setters, the Gordon will correctly tend to single track as its speed increases. This breed must move with free, naturally graceful, effortless strides.

Photo by Ashbey.[viii]

Examining the Dog

The purpose of competitive exhibition by dedicated breeders is to obtain an assessment of the individual dog as compared to the details in the standard. It is therefore essential that every person attempting to judge or assess the Gordon knows and understands the standard. Keeping in mind that this is an endurance hunter and must conform to the Gordon silhouette (see page 72), start with a general impression of the group of dogs. Which comes closest to the ideal in appearance? Which dogs meet the criteria for color and markings; which ones cover ground while maintaining correct style and shape? Which are too large, too small, and too similar to another setter?

The dogs that are correct will need to be evaluated in detail and then compared to each other. The dogs that do not as closely approach the standard will have to be examined to find out why they are faulty and to what degree.

Gordon Setter Male. Photo by Tath.

Vertical and horizontal assessment (see diagram, page 73). Next comes the overview of the individual specimen. A vertical assessment includes the proportions from withers to foot and the placement of parts that should conform to straight lines. One should pay attention, for example, to the following proportions and alignments: The distance from the withers to the elbow should be about equal to the distance from the elbow to the ground. The line drawn from the withers straight down and perpendicular to the ground should pass through the elbow joint down the back of the leg and slightly to the rear of the pastern and foot. To indicate vertical balance in the rear, a straight line should pass through the point of the buttock or ischeum and should end several inches in front of the rear foot. Another vertical line parallels the back of the hock, illustrating its upright position. These visual estimates must be checked against the topline to assure that it is level and against the rear leg to check for the correct bend in the stifle.

The horizontal assessment of the Gordon Setter includes the proportions of body length. The line from the withers to the buttocks creates the top of a rectangle that is approximately square. Thus, the line from the point of the shoulder (forechest) to the buttocks forms the top of a rectangle that is longer than it is high. The AKC standard calls for the Gordon Setter to be more square in body measurement. In other countries the standards describe the Gordon as longer in body than it is high.

However, no amount of visualizing and estimating is enough. It is essential to get one's hands on the dog. Examine the head and the bite, evaluate the characteristic markings, and check for parallel planes of the muzzle and skull from both the front and the side. Examine the neck from the arch to the withers and examine the front of the neck to find the point of the shoulder. The positioning of the dog by the handler and the presentation of the trimming may create false lines. Are the ribs angled back? Where is the last rib? How wide and deep is the chest? Only by hand examination can the loin be evaluated properly—it should be well muscled and firm. The pelvis

Puppies

Photo courtesy of Dean and Jane Matteson.

Photo by Ferguson.

Photo courtesy of Jane Matteson.

should be long and substantial as it determines the performance of the rear assembly. Check for the bend at the stifle joint and assess the length of the lower thigh. Feel the shape and firmness of the hock—the hock must be short. From the rear of the dog examine the muscling of the upper and lower thighs.

While cognitively processing and evaluating what the examination has brought to light, take notice of the coat— color, texture and type of hair. The original Gordon was never designed to have coat resembling an American Cocker Spaniel or an English Sheepdog. There should be no wooliness that tends to appear frizzy and distorts the shape and lines of the setter. In the last twenty years both heavy texture and excessive length of Gordon coats have made examination of dogs more difficult. Unfortunately, an uncharacteristic coat has been bred into our dogs and has become an impediment to grooming and maintenance for the pet owner, the show enthusiast, and the hunter. The coat should be silky, as straight as possible, and shining. Finally, an evaluation of tail and tail carriage must be included. The Gordon Setter tail should be short and should never measure beyond the hock joint. The internationally accepted tail carriage for a Gordon Setter is at the level of the back, as indicative of a happy, willing disposition. Although American judges tend to forgive the gay tail, the AKC standard does not so instruct them.

The discussion of the Gordon Setter—temperament, conformation, movement, and evaluation—is by no means all-inclusive; yet it should serve the Gordon fancier, breeder, exhibitor, and judge as either a starting point or a review.

The Gordon Setter must possess the characteristics of a competent gun dog. The shiny black straight coat must be trouble free and uniquely attractive in contrast with the deep chestnut markings. Correct balance in a standing position and smooth, strong coordinated motion is the essence of this magnificent dog from Scotland.

Photo courtesy of Dean and Jane Matteson.

Gordon Setter on Point.

Gordon Setter and Pheasant.
Photo by Donna Carson.

Gordon Setter Pedigree

The following examples of pedigrees are offered as an instructional guide for students of the breed. They tell a fascinating story of breed origins, constitute a paradigm of outcrossing and linebreeding, and remind the serious breeder that significant contributions have been made by those of years gone by. The first example, the pedigree of Can. & Amer. Ch. Sangerfield Patsy, CD shows the consistent and close linebreeding of this famous New York State kennel. Ch. Sangerfield Tracy figures six times in the third generation. In addition, Patsy's sire, Can.& Am. Ch. Sporting Look is the combination of a half-brother/half-sister (their sire is Ch. Sangerfield Index).

In examining pedigrees of forty years ago it is rare to find a kennel that did not have an Afternod Gordon. Heslop and Sangerfield were primary breeders as well. As a result of these great kennels of the past new kennels were able to begin with fine, well bred individuals that were the product of years of careful programs.

The second example is a pedigree from Australia that shows the native Gordons before the era of American imports. The first two Gordons arrived in Australia around 1860. Their names were Ponto and Dido and they came from a reputable kennel in the Isle of Skye. Three more Gordon Setters came from the United Kingdom in 1889 from the Heather Kennels. Imports from New Zealand arrived in the early twentieth century which originally had come from British kennels. The first field trial champion in New South Wales was Glenhaig Trigger. The O'Argyles were famous in the 1920's and 1930's and were remembered as fine dogs by C. Bede Maxwell. Line breeding was a necessity not a choice because new bloodlines did not exist especially after the death of George Edwards, the two world wars, and the very strict quarantine laws. By the 1960's The State of Victoria became the source of breeding stock for new kennels. Julie Dickenson imported two Gordons from New Zealand with the bitch in whelp. One of the get became the foundation for Warchant—Ch. Lorroy Scot Robin. In 1970 Esther Joseph acquired a bitch from the old Victorian bloodlines which began the Triseter Gordons of today.

The third example is the complete outcross of the extradinary strength of the British-Victorian lines with the Gordon from the United States imported by Graeme Lack and his daughter Jayne—Ch.Sutherland Hallmark. This campact yet well angled and well coated Gordon introduced the necessary qualities that Australian breeders were looking for. Guy was a great producer, a spirited showman, and a proven field trialer. Notice his pedigree goes back to key lines in the United States: Sutherland, Loch Adair and, of course, Afternod.

Gordon Setter Pedigree

Can. & U.S Ch. Sangerfield Patsy, CD
Whelped November 5, 1967

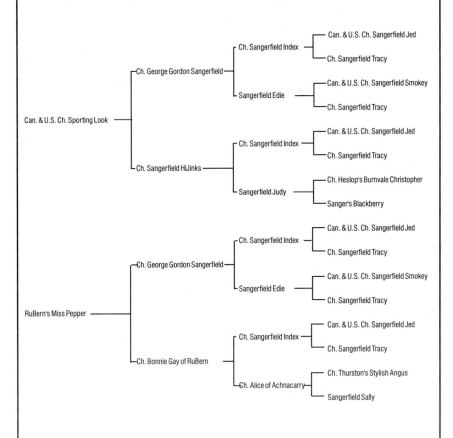

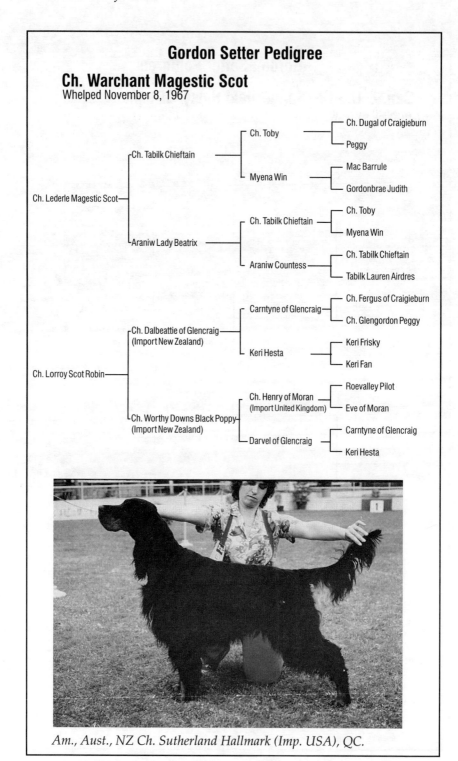

Gordon Setter Pedigree

Ch. Warchant Magestic Scot
Whelped November 8, 1967

- Ch. Lederle Magestic Scot
  - Ch. Tabilk Chieftain
    - Ch. Toby
      - Ch. Dugal of Craigieburn
      - Peggy
    - Myena Win
      - Mac Barrule
      - Gordonbrae Judith
  - Araniw Lady Beatrix
    - Ch. Tabilk Chieftain
      - Ch. Toby
      - Myena Win
    - Araniw Countess
      - Ch. Tabilk Chieftain
      - Tabilk Lauren Airdres
- Ch. Lorroy Scot Robin
  - Ch. Dalbeattie of Glencraig
    (Import New Zealand)
    - Carntyne of Glencraig
      - Ch. Fergus of Craigieburn
      - Ch. Glengordon Peggy
    - Keri Hesta
      - Keri Frisky
      - Keri Fan
  - Ch. Worthy Downs Black Poppy
    (Import New Zealand)
    - Ch. Henry of Moran
      (Import United Kingdom)
      - Roevalley Pilot
      - Eve of Moran
    - Darvel of Glencraig
      - Carntyne of Glencraig
      - Keri Hesta

Am., Aust., NZ Ch. Sutherland Hallmark (Imp. USA), QC.

Gordon Setter Pedigree

Triseter Black Annwen
Whelped March 11, 1976

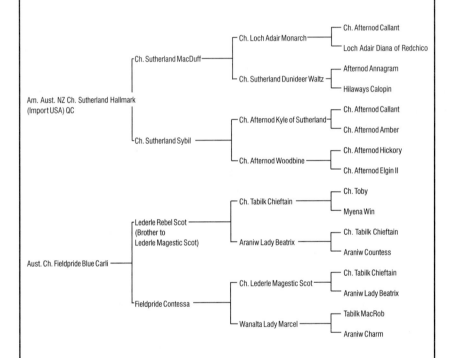

Outcross: *the mating of unrelated individuals*

Inbreeding: *a type of breeding program employed to obtain improvements and/or "fix" desirable physical and/or mental attributes through the mating of closely related stock such as sister/brother, father/daughter, etc.*

Linebreeding: *The concentration of characteristics of an individual or strain with an attempt to keep inbreeding at a minimum. The mating of two dogs related by direct descent.*

Photo Endnotes

i.   Courtesy of the Chevalier Collection.

ii.   Art Bains handling Ch. Afternod Ripple for owner Carol Chevalier.

iii. Ch. Craig of Redchico, son of Ch. Afternod Drambuie.

iv.   An ideal bitch head Ch. Afternod Example.

v.   Am. & Can. Ch. MacAlder Mister Chips.

vi.   Ch. MacAlder Penelope.

vii. Ch. Buteo's Colorado.

viii. Am. & Can. Ch. Gordonhill Casa Blanca.

4 The Irish Red and White Setter

by Patricia Brigden

*O*ver the last one hundred and fifty years setters have exhibited a steady process of divergence. The English and Gordon were developed in specific ways to suit the terrain for which they were intended and to satisfy the hunting requirements of the place and the time. The Irish Setter and the Irish Red and White Setter, although considered one breed in the register of the Irish Kennel Club until as late as 1980, have also traveled separate paths.

Setters of Ireland have been documented with certainty from the seventeenth century. Famous paintings have recorded the greats and the near greats with their favorite possessions— including their dogs. Evidence indicates the emergence of a setter with a white body with red markings, and the same type setter of solid coloured red. According to the Leighton-Boyce research, twentieth century arguments suggest that the setter type dog in a self-portrait by Bacon in 1626 depicts a setter— and a red and white setter at that[1]. Certainly, the evidence of the setter that appears in solid red in the Van Dyck painting of 1634 (see color plate 3) is compelling.

Yet to place too much importance on these unique evidences may mislead the reader of the setter story. The setters of Ireland were developed as a practical necessity to find game for the hunter in a land where that game was not always plentiful. The skill of the dog as a hunter was primary, and

Patricia Brigden at Autumnwood House.

individual dogs were bred from to establish a working setter. Although no specific examples exist, it is widely held that, "During the seventeenth century and for the next hundred years, dogs from Spain and the low countries, possibly brought by officers in the armies returning from the continent, were interbred with the indigenous stock."[2] And because pointers were known to have entered Britain at this time, it is a reasonable inference that this type of hunter may also have figured in the ancestry of the setters of Ireland.[3]

The colour of these dogs in the early development of the breed was probably of little consequence. The colour simply was the common link to the ancient spaniels that were white with red patches (see color plate 4). But during the Eighteenth century, colour did become an important point of identification for this setter as it evolved in Ireland. Paintings in Ireland and England inform us of the existence of this gundog whose coat was in most cases white with deep red patches. It is also known that an entirely red setter and the red setter with a white blaze and other traces of white appeared in greater numbers from the late 1700's until the era of the first dog shows. "At the Rotunda Show in Dublin in 1863 both colours of Irish Setter were shown" ...but this date also marked a time after which the popularity of the Irish Red Setter as a solid coloured dog was established.[4]

While it is essential to explain briefly the beginnings of the setters of Ireland, and interesting to document that white setters with deep red patches existed in significant numbers prior to the solid coloured dogs, it is the primary purpose of this chapter to describe the Irish Red and White Setter, which we today recognize as a separate breed. The divergence of type between the two Irish Setter strains widened as a result of the setter's usefulness, the dog show, the field trial, and the aesthetic demands of popular fancy. The working red setters and red and whites found on farms in Ireland or used as shooting companions were sturdier in build than the lean red dogs used for field trials and the red dogs that became so popular at dog shows. The red show dogs seen in Irish and English exhibition

Photo by Brigden.

2001. Photo courtesy of Bateman.[i] Photo by John Hartley.

rings became more elegant during the century following the first established shows. These setters had longer necks and heavier feathered coats. They were different from the practical, strong, stocky Red and White Setters that remained on the farms and in the fields and bogs of Ireland carrying on their ancient work. Also, demands from sportsmen in the United States for the red setter as a show dog and field trial competitor grew, and the breed on American soil took a path of even greater diversity. The Irish Setter that was commonly known in the United States became taller, more glamorous in coat and style, and was bred to be more exaggerated in lines and proportions when compared to the show dogs in Ireland and England.

This, then, left the Irish Red and White Setter in less demand, with less popular support and, because they were judged under the same standard as the Irish Red Setter, in a precarious position as a show competitor. In fact, by the beginning of the twentieth century the Red and White Setter was sparse in numbers and was not even identified as a known breed or variety in the United States.

Irish Red & White Setters at Swords Championship Show, 1982.
Photo by Brigden.

Two major revivals have occurred to save the breed from extinction—one in the 1940's and the more recent in the late 1970's. Of significance, of course, was the action of the Irish Kennel Club in 1980 in separating the two breeds of Irish Setter by approving a standard for the ancient yet revived breed. The British Kennel Club followed soon after with their standard, which was similar to that formulated in the country.

Irish breeders had in fact devoted themselves to finding individual dogs that were either obviously red and white, or that were solid coloured but carried traces of white. A breeding program was set up, litter inspections were carried out and the resulting setters began to conform to the desired characteristics. British fanciers also aided in the revival by importing small numbers of dogs from Ireland and by working diligently to broaden the breeding base. By the mid 1980's Irish Red and Whites were also exported to North America and Australasia.

Today, these setters compete in Commonwealth countries and at international shows, while in the United States these parti-coloured setters compete only in shows sponsored by the American Rare Breeds Association. However, the Irish Red and

White Setter Club of America has been organized, has adopted a breed standard, publishes a regular newsletter, holds a yearly national specialty show, and has submitted application to the American Kennel Club for admission as Miscellaneous Class status.

Clearly the breed has made considerable progress in a short period of time, but the real measure of success stands in the future. This setter is still limited in numbers and gene pool; individual lines are scattered all over the globe; and the pillars of the revival stage, those who taught others by word and experience, will in the future be replaced by fanciers who cannot know nor appreciate either the characteristics of the stock or the re-establishment process. Still, the written standards offer clear guidelines. What they call for and how the envisioned type differs from the other setters will be explored under the headings of temperament, physical appearance, coat and colour, and the dog in motion will follow.

Temperament

It must be emphasized that these setters are highly intelligent members of the canine species. Not only have they consistently demonstrated an understanding for a sizable vocabulary, but it is common for Red and Whites to master such tasks as opening a crate from the inside as well as from the outside, as well as a refrigerator, gate, or door. With its inherent curiosity and intelligence, this is a dog that can get into mischief if allowed to do so. And although such skills around the house are not always appreciated by owners, these dogs excel at Obedience, Agility, and field work. Besides, Red and Whites are excellent family dogs; they make grand companions for children because they are trustworthy and loving, yet also energetic and playful. The Red and White credo appears to be that "every day is a day to be enjoyed". As is true with many among the other setter breeds, this dog flourishes as a house dog and does not take well to kennel life. They are happiest when they can build rapport with family members and although they are alert to the arrival of strangers, they tend to be receptive to a wide variety of people, and therefore cannot

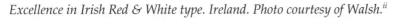

Excellence in Irish Red & White type. Ireland. Photo courtesy of Walsh.[ii]

Irish Red & White Setters must be of sound temperament and flexible to accept a wide variety of human relationships and situations.

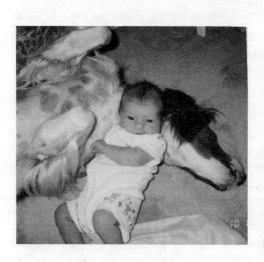

Mairin Daly with Ch. Bairre, Ireland. Courtesy of Canon Patrick Doherty.

Photo by G. Bayne.[iii]

be considered competent guard dogs. When the original work of the Red and White is considered—a dog hunting out of earshot of its owner, a dog responding to hand signals or whistles, a dog in control but able to think beyond its instincts—it is not so remarkable that today's dogs are attentive, curious and intelligent.

Physical Characteristics

The intentions of the breeders who worked so hard to preserve this setter are very clear in the words from the Irish standard: " The Irish Red and White Setter is bred primarily for the field. The standard as set out hereunder must be interpreted chiefly from this point of view and all Judges and Bench shows must be encouraged to judge the exhibits chiefly from the working standpoint." In addition, the new owner, breeder and judge must understand and follow the guidelines of the British Kennel Club (England) and the Irish Kennel Club standards when they call for a strong and powerful dog that is athletic rather than racy. This is meant to distinguish between the two Irish Setters. While the whole coloured dog is to be of

A well made Red & White bitch.[iv] California.

Head Study Irish Red & White Setter

Head Study Irish Red & White Setter

Ireland. Photo courtesy of Trudy Walsh.

Courtesy of Bellavanti.ᵛ Photo by S. Domun.

elegant lines with a look of speed, the Red and White is to be a practical, durable, working hunter whose beauty is derived from balance, strength and proportion.

The head is certainly the breed's most unique characteristic and its fine points are going to require instruction for future generations of breeders and judges. It must not look like the other setters and it must be evaluated without the artificial renderings of traditional setter grooming. For example, the head—like the overall appearance of the dog—must be understood in its own right, and not according to what one's experience from another setter breed would like it to be. Further, the dog must be presented with its natural coat intact. The American Standard is the most detailed here, with clear instructions on the natural appearance of the neck ruff, the presence of whiskers, and the essential feathering on the top of the ears. The head should be broad (from ear to ear) in proportion to the body and as a result the muzzle often appears to be shorter than the skull when, in fact, the two should be of equal length. The muzzle is clear cut without the flews common to the English and Gordon Setter. In the British and the Irish

Courtesy of Raykes. Pennsylvania.

© PDETMOLD
2001

Silhouette of the Irish Red & White Setter

Irish Red and White Setter

*The Irish Red and White Setter is level in topline or may appear slightly sloping because the ruff of coat covering the shoulders gives the **impression** of more height at the withers than at the rear (protuberance at the top of the upper pelvis). The head is unique and should not be compared to the other setters. Although the skull and muzzle are equal in length, the size and width of the skull as compared to the narrower width of the muzzle may create an impression that the muzzle is shorter. The presence of the occiput should be identified by touch but there is not a definition to be seen. The flews neatly cover the under jaw creating a tapered muzzle that is squared off at the end. Because the neck is to be left in a natural growth of coat it may appear shorter. Although the Red and White is slightly shorter in height than the English Setter, it will appear smaller because it carries less bone. The Red and White also appears smaller because it **correctly** carries much less length of coat. The balance between the running gear of front and rear is essential. What cannot be seen in the silhouette is the well-sprung rib cage which is larger than the other setters when evaluated in proportion to the whole dog. Legs are strong, feet are small and firm, and the development of bone is durable but is less in mass than the other setters. The tail, which is to be naturally coated, may appear longer than it actually is. This silhouette is an overall picture but the dog must be carefully examined by hand to assess its structure. (Exact wording of the standard is in the appendix).*

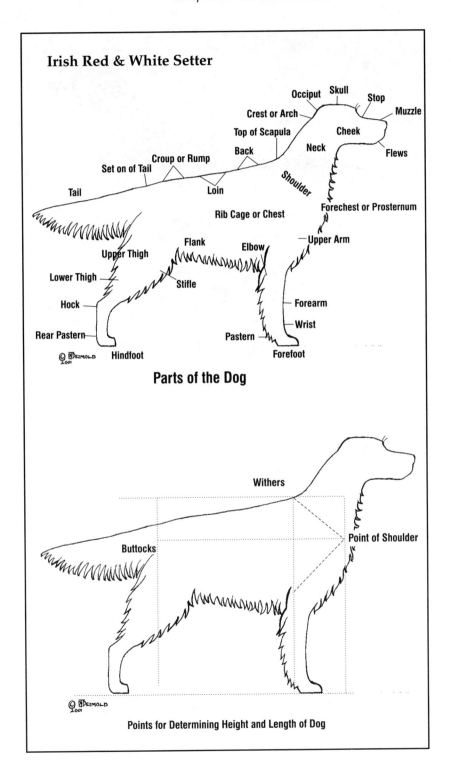

Irish Red & White Setter

Parts of the Dog

Points for Determining Height and Length of Dog

*2000. Mrs. W.A.J. Iles with Glennessa Irish Red & White Setters. England.
Photo by Iles-Hebbert.*

Standard a domed skull is called for, along with a back skull
that is free from a visible definition of occipital protuberance.
It is important to note here, however, that the American Standard describes a moderate stop in the fore-face and a skull that
is **not** domed. From the side the head appears heavy in skull
and light in muzzle. From the front the dog must look alert and
intelligent.

The body of the Red and White Setter is designed to be a
working machine. The dog must have an ample, well-sprung
rib cage and a good depth of chest. In proportion to the dog's
general size and bone, the rib cage should appear well developed but not barrel-shaped, and never slender and racy. While
forequarters and hindquarters must be strong, well angled,
and muscular, the legs are to be straight, strong and sinewy. In

other words, the leg bones are oval not round and they have the appearance of athletic ability. The feet of the Red and White are small, close-knit and in proportion to this lighter weight setter. The American standard differs from the British and Irish standards in calling for a round foot. A proper balance between the front and rear angles is key to the functioning of a capable working setter. The silhouette of the dog must include a headpiece of modest length, a naturally coated, well arched neck, a level, strong back and a tail set and carriage that is either at the level of the back or lower. Because the breed is to be presented in a manner free from artificial trimming, the tail may appear longer than it actually is. Although the dog must look agile and capable of speed, the Red and White's characteristics include a skull of breadth and substance and a rib cage that is more ample than that of the Irish Red Setter. The dog stands with confidence, eager to please, and appears slightly longer than it is high.

Photo by G. Bayne.[vi]

Coat, Colour, and Markings

1994 Irish Red & White Setter and Irish Setter. Photo by Lori Stewart.

The crowning glory of the Red and White Setter is its magnificent coat. The dog should always give the first impression of being a white dog with clearly defined red "islands" or patches. The colours of the coat should look alive and in a healthy bloom. While all the standards are specific and in agreement about the areas where mottling or flecking may occur (only on the face and feet up to the elbow and up to the hock), the American Standard offers details about the quality of the colour: the white is to be a **pure** white, not flat, and with a pearly shine, and the red is to be a rich, deep red or chestnut indicative of its Irish origins. Also the nose is described as black or dark brown, the lip pigment black or dark brown and the eye rim pigment from dark pinkish brown to black. Other markings are understood to be important to the breed's appearance although they are not included in the standards. A patch over both eyes is expected, the ears are to be red, and the flash or blaze of white down the fore-face is a breed characteristic. There should be at least one clear red patch on each side of the body and a spot at the root of the tail. Also common and

Puppies

the delight of many breeders is the "thumbprint" or spot of red on the top of the skull about the size of a 50 pence piece.

The coat must be straight and flat and the feathering is to be moderate and silky, appearing on the outer flap of the ear, the back of the legs, and beneath the tail. The coat under the body is described as a fringe and is to be moderate. The Red and White does not live up to its name when it is roaned, ginger, orange, or brown; and it is incorrectly marked when the patches bleed into the white or the patches become a saddle or larger marking.

The Dog in Motion

The anatomical parts of the Irish Red and White Setter call for a dog that is in all ways a working gun dog. A dog that is built correctly, and, of course, in good condition, and good health, will move with a long, free striding, effortless, and lively gait. When in motion the dog should carry its head high and keep its feet low. In other words, the setter uses its nose for winding, not for following a ground trail. And the dog uses its properly constructed forequarters, hindquarters and legs in an effortless manner in which the feet stay close to the ground. It must be noted that the description in the standards refers to the dog in motion at a trot in the show ring. A thorough study

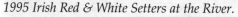

1995 Irish Red & White Setters at the River.

Dogs in Motion.[vii]

Irish Champion Meudon Blaze and Irish Champion Mount Eagle Belle. From the private collection of Canon Patrick Doherty.

of all three standards will help the breeder and judge to understand the method of evaluation. However, it is necessary to remember that this dog is an all-day hunter that must use the gallop to cover ground and quarter the field. The Red and White, therefore must also be well endowed with a strong back, loin, feet, and pasterns to carry out turns and jumps during the gallop. Finally, the dog must have the strength and width of rear assembly to work efficiently with and around the rounded rib cage and the width of the forequarters.

This, then is the Irish Red and White Setter. It is a breed well documented prior to the advent of the dog show, and a breed now experiencing re-birth and recognition around the world. Long preserved by Irish farmers and hunters, it only recently came under the guardianship of the show fanciers, and today the Irish Red and White Setter and its devoted owners look to a bright future in both show ring and field.

Killarney Championship Show, Ireland, 1991. Courtesy of Canon Patrick Doherty.

Irish Red & White Setter, George, owned by Maureen Cuddy. 1979.

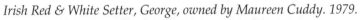

*1997 Canon Patrick Doherty with his Irish Red & White Setter,
County Kerry, Ireland.*

First and foremost the Irish Red & White Setter must have the working potential of an active gundog.

Photo courtesy of Criss. California.

Photo courtesy of Wallace-Jones.

Irish Red and White Setter Pedigree

The following examples of pedigrees are offered as instructional charts for students of the breed. They tell an important history of a line and together with information about individual dogs in the pedigree, provide the breeder with a guide to the future. The pedigrees of Gameshot of Autumnwood and Harlequin of Knockalla are key to the revival of the breed. From these lines flow the present day Red and Whites around the world. The third pedigree is offered as an example of a combination of breeding programs from England on one side and from Ireland on the other that produced a first generation in the United States.

Gameshot of Autumnwood

Whelped May 31, 1981

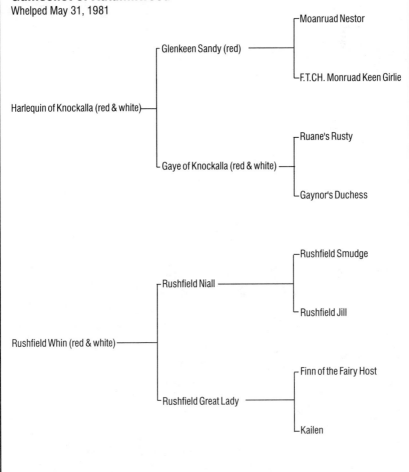

Irish Red & White Setter Pedigree

Harlequin of Knockalla
Whelped April 4, 1977

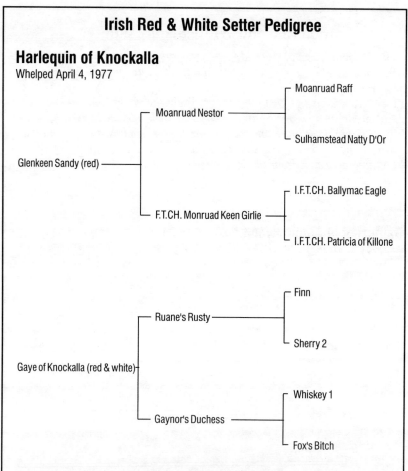

- Glenkeen Sandy (red)
  - Moanruad Nestor
    - Moanruad Raff
    - Sulhamstead Natty D'Or
  - F.T.CH. Monruad Keen Girlie
    - I.F.T.CH. Ballymac Eagle
    - I.F.T.CH. Patricia of Killone
- Gaye of Knockalla (red & white)
  - Ruane's Rusty
    - Finn
    - Sherry 2
  - Gaynor's Duchess
    - Whiskey 1
    - Fox's Bitch

Irish Red & White Ch. Harlequin of Knockalla. Photo by Brigden. 1984.

Irish Red & White Setter Pedigree

American-Bred Litter
Whelped March 18, 1998

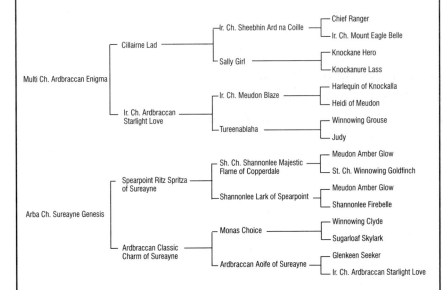

Outcross: the mating of unrelated individuals

Inbreeding: a type of breeding program employed to obtain improvements and/or "fix" desirable physical and/or mental attributes through the mating of closely related stock such as sister/brother, father/daughter, etc.

Linebreeding: *The concentration of characteristics of an individual or strain with an attempt to keep inbreeding at a minimum. The mating of two dogs related by direct descent.*

Endnotes

1   Leighton-Boyce, Gilbert. *A Survey of Early Setters.* 1985, London.

2   Brigden, Patricia. *The Irish Red and White Setter.* 1997, 2nd Edition. England.

3   Ibid.

4   Ibid.

Photo Endnotes

i.   Cormallen Sparkling Light.

ii.   Champion Ardbraccan Dunboyne.

iii. Irish Red & White Setters of Corranroo. England.

iv.   Ch. Sureayne Genesis.

v.   UK and Irish Ch. Bellavanti Beachcomber.

vi.   Courtesy of Corranroo Kennels, England.

vii. Photos courtesy of Patsy Wallace-Jones. California.

viii. (ARBA) Mex., F.C.I. Ch. Ardbraccan Enigma (Junior Hunter test passed). Owned by Wallace.

Photo by R.S. Brown. California.[viii]

5 | The Irish Setter

by John Savory

The essence of the Irish Setter and its breed characteristics are intimately reflected in its original purpose as a highly active gundog. From the tip of the nose to the end of the tail, all physical and mental characteristics of the Irish Setter play a role in the success of a breed whose original function was finding game birds. Originally the Irish Setter hunted over countryside and moorland less rugged than that worked by his cousin the Gordon Setter, and with less undergrowth than where the English Setter was originally used. The open and wide-ranging terrain over which the Irish Setter hunted influenced the structure of the breed. The Irish Setter must be capable of hunting all day with great enthusiasm and stamina in country where birds might not be plentiful, and repeating the job the next day and the one after. He must be substantial without being cumbersome. A dog with too much size would not have the endurance for the task in hand; a smaller specimen would lack the capability to cover sufficient ground to have a successful day in the field. This explanation and analysis of the essential characteristics of the Irish Setter will be presented in three parts: temperament, physical characteristics, and movement.

Irish Elegance in California.[i] Photo by Haigler.

Temperament

Fundamental to the success of the Irish Setter as a gundog is temperament, particularly the relationship to the hunter and master. It is described to perfection in Tolstoy's *Anna Karenina*. When one of the main characters returns to his country estate after an extended absence, "A setter bitch, Laska, ran out too, and whining, turned around Levin's knees, jumping up and longing, but not daring, to put her forepaws on his chest". And later, "Laska kept poking her head under his hand. He stroked her, and she promptly curled up at his feet, laying her head on a hind paw. And in token of all now being well and satisfactory, she opened her mouth a little, smacked her lips, and settling her sticky lips more comfortably about her old teeth, she sank into blissful repose. Levin watched all her movements attentively....Nothing's amiss....All's well". On the following day we again see the faithful dog "...who with one ear raised, wagged the end of her shaggy tail, came slowly back as though she would prolong the pleasure, and as it were smiling, brought the dead bird to her master." Tolstoy does not specify that the dog is an Irish Setter, but surely his words describe the loving temperament and keen hunting ability that are all-important features of this beautiful breed.

Another event testifying to the solid, dependable temperament of the Irish Setter shared by many Irish Setter breeders
and exhibitors occurred at the Irish Setter Club of America
National Specialty in Warwick, Rhode Island in June, 1997. In
the middle of the night following the Thursday judging, there
was a violent thunderstorm during which lightning struck the
host hotel, triggering the fire alarms. Since most of the exhibitors and dogs were located in the hotel, there was a great deal
of anxiety, particularly since jammed stairwells prevented
timely exit. Yet despite the commotion, the intensity of the
thunder and lightning, and the unnerving din of the fire alarm
the dogs were calm and orderly. No growling or aggressive-
ness was seen and most of the dogs maintained a calmer
demeanor than their worried owners. Even outside in the foul
weather, the dogs remained under control. This experience
demonstrated to all of us present that we could be proud that
our breed had been developed with such wonderful disposi-
tions. We owe a debt to the breeders of past generations who
produced the tranquil temperament of our present-day dogs.

John Savory judging Best in Specialty Show, Victoria, Australia.[ii]

Photo by Michael.[iii]

Temperament and Instinct

The Irish Setter is indeed an exuberant hunter, being all muscle and energy in the field, ready to hunt from dawn until dusk, never tiring or losing interest even when birds are difficult to find. Like the other setters, the Irish Setter traces its ancestry to dogs used to locate birds which were then captured by netting. Denlinger[1] in his early book on the Irish Setter refers to the first book ever written on dogs, *Of Englishe Dogges*[2] by Johannes Caius (1576) who describes working in this manner...

> When he hath founde the byrde, he keepeth sure and fast silence, he stayeth his steppes and wil proceede no further, and with a close couert watching eye, layeth his belly to the grounde and so creepeth forward like a worme. When he approcheth neere to the place where the birde is, he layes him downe, and with a marcke of his pawes, betrayeth the place of the byrdes last abode, wherby it is supposed that this kinde of

dogge is called Index, Setter, being in deede a name most consonant and agreable to his quality. The place being knowne by the meanes of the dogge, the fowler immediatly openeth and spreedeth his net, intending to take them, which being done the dogge at the accustomed becke or vsuall signe of his Master ryseth vp by and by, and draweth neerer to the fowle that by his presence they might be the authors of their owne insnaring, and be ready intangled in the prepared net....

This description of its predecessor provides a basis for understanding the form of the present day Irish Setter. A long shoulder blade, fine but not too narrow at the points, and a well-angled rear are beneficial structural features for a dog whose mode of hunting requires stamina, stealth, and crouching. These features certainly proved to be of considerable

Irish Setter as a Companion.[iv]

*Photo courtesy of the McAteer
collection. 1948.*[v]

importance in the later development of the gundog in the
latter half of the eighteenth century.

While the quotations from Tolstoy and Caius apply generally to the setter breeds, they provide an excellent basis for
elucidating the temperament and instinct of the Irish Setter.
The standard calls for "a rollicking personality" and this fits
the breed perfectly. The energy and enthusiasm of the Irish
Setter is depicted superbly in the Haycock print[3] (Color Plate
22) where the artist has captured the intensity of the Irish
Setter at work and their serious dedication to the task. Yet the
Irish Setter temperament is flexible: loyalty and dependability
must go beyond the relationship with the hunter to include
family members. Children develop with these loyal and trustworthy dogs relationships that are not diminished through the
years.

Physical Characteristics

The silhouettes of the four setters are truly distinctive (see page 216). The Irish Setter is the tallest, and the eye of the beholder is immediately drawn to the pleasing symmetry of its lines. The angle of the slope from the withers to the croup is greater in the Irish Setter than the others. This slope results both from a long shoulder blade that is angled well back but slightly more upright than the other setters, combined with a depth of turn at the stifles and hocks. These features are of great importance in allowing the Irish Setter to run effortlessly using both the trot and, more important, the gallop for hours on end in search of game. The long lean head that the ancients described as "shallow-flewed", is uniquely Irish, allows for adequate brain room without being too large, and provides the structure for the efficient olfactory system so important in locating game birds. The overall silhouette of the Irish Setter is of a dog up on leg, slender and strong, with sloping top line, lean and aristocratic head, and the look of a competent, fast moving gun dog.

Irish Setters should always have an "angle". Photo by Ludwig.[vi]

Tri-State Specialty, 1953 with Paula McAteer and Joe Knight. [vii]
Photo by Shafer

Famous breeder, writer, and judge Lee Schoen presenting the ribbon. [viii]

Besides depicting overall excellence of form, the silhouettes indicate differences between males and females. The dog is the more substantial, with slightly more bone and a more substantial head. The bitch is not lacking in substance, but illustrates more refinement. Looking at the two examples of Irish Setters, it should be easy to distinguish the dogs from the bitches. Although the Irish, English, Gordon, and Irish Red & White Setters obviously have many similarities in the head, there are nevertheless marked differences. Above all, the head of the Irish Setter is lean and long and in proportion to the size of the whole animal. The length should be at least double the width between the ears, and as stated by Eldredge and Vanacore[4] "the proportions of the head are what make it distinctive and certainly set it apart from the English or Gordon Setter". The classic description of "brick on brick" provides a good basis for explaining the head, since the planes of the muzzle and skull should be parallel, and a distinct stop must be evident. The two pages of head studies help illustrate excellent parallel planes and good stop. Too much stop, however, is unattractive and detracts from a soft and kind expression. Additionally, the muzzle should have sufficient width, approaching that of the

Photo by Nilsen.[ix]

Head Study: Irish Setters

x

xi

Head studies on these pages include dogs and bitches from California, Massachusetts, Minnesota, New York, and Melbourne, Australia.

Excellence in Juniors. 1970.[xii]

backskull, and with these features the nose should be relatively large with wide nostrils allowing for an efficient
olfactory system; this is vital for the dog to scent game. The
backskull should be level and must not drop off at the rear. The
head is finished by delicate chiseling on the muzzle so that the
area beneath the eyes is flat and free from fill. This not only
enhances the field of vision, but provides an aesthetic touch
worthy of a fine sculptor. The eyes of the Irish Setter are almond-
shaped, open, intelligent, and placed well apart to enhance
vision, and are dark to medium brown. Light eyes detract from
the expression as do eyes that are slanting or squinting. Their
expression should be soft but alert. Leather thin ears set well
back and low on the skull are typical of the Irish Setter and add
greatly to the framing of the expression. A soft, loving, intelligent and alert expression is truly an important component of
the Irish Setter. Indeed, as the Irish Setter ages, the head achieves
an even greater elegance which results from a thinning of the
facial muscles and a graying of the facial hair. It is a look that
brings back a flood of memories and tugs at the heartstrings.

The neck of the Irish Setter is in accord with the overall nobility and function of this breed. A long, slightly arched and strong neck must be in sensible proportion with the rest of the body. The correct neck brings the center of gravity forward at the right time during the gallop, a feature of vital importance in achieving an efficient and correct gait. A longish neck also aids in the retrieval of game and, as indicated earlier, must have been a significant structural feature in the remote ancestors who were used as netting dogs. Measured from the junction with the head to the point of the withers, the neck can be of good length only when the layback of the shoulder is angled toward the back. The neck must be well muscled since it plays a role in movement, and it must fit smoothly into the shoulders without any indication of protuberance from a faulty upright scapula.

The body of the Irish Setter befits a dog which must have extraordinary endurance. As with dogs in general, the most difficult aspect of this breed to understand is the front assembly and front movement. The well developed front allows room for a long, deep, tapered, oval rib cage, yet it must be narrow enough to accommodate a wide powerful rear at the gallop. In fact, the Irish Setter is more a galloping than a trotting dog when at work. In the show ring, therefore, where the trot is the gait used to assess movement, the evaluation should assess how this gait reflects the efficiency of the gallop. Long, wide shoulder blades that slope well back are very important to the breed. A forty-five degree angle is the ideal, but seldom quite attainable. The shoulders meet fairly close together at the withers but not so close as to interfere with the ability of the dog to reach and retrieve game. Correct layback of the shoulders invariably leads to good neck placement, creating a smooth line at the juction. The upper arm and shoulder blade meet sufficiently forward so as to suggest good depth of chest, and the angle of the upper arm approaches ninety degrees. A long upper arm is essential for reach both at the trot and gallop. The length of the upper arm does not quite achieve the length of the shoulder blade, however, even though the shoulder blade may appear to be longer because of size and shape.

Silhouette of Irish Setter

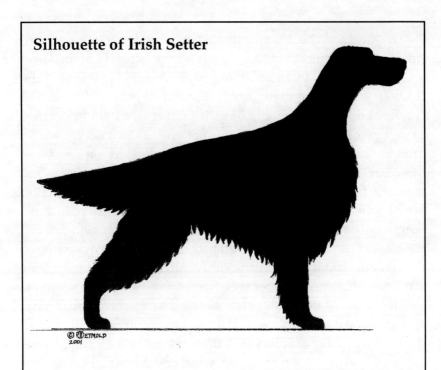

The Irish Setter

The Irish Setter is sloping in topline and is slightly longer than it is high. The head is long, lean, and clean in lines. The skull and muzzle are close to the same width and are equal in length. The planes of the head and muzzle must be parallel. The flews cover neatly the development of the lower jaw and end in a squared end of the muzzle. Development of the forechest or prosternum is essential. The angulation of the front is deep so that the forelegs are set well under the dog and the line of the shoulder blade is sloped well back. The balance of the rearquarters with the front requires that the rear be correctly constructed without exaggerated length of any part of the assembly. The Irish must look as a dog standing over plenty of ground: Legs are long, strong and lean, feet are rather small. Standing naturally, the Irish must have short hocks that are perpendicular to the ground. The tail is presented as an extension of the sloping topline and is held slightly lower than the set on of the tail. It should be carried level or very slightly elevated as allowed in the American standard. (Exact wording of the standards is in the appendix).

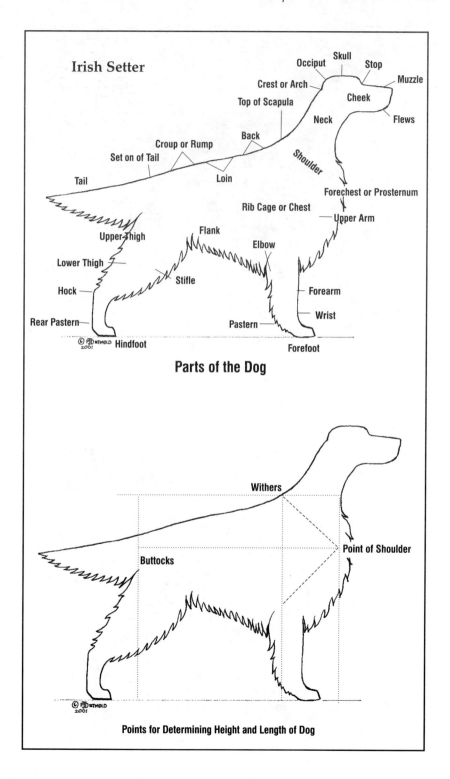

Parts of the Dog

Points for Determining Height and Length of Dog

Ideal Irish Setter Male. [xiii] *Photo by Nilsen.*

Ideal Irish Setter Bitch. Courtesy of John Savory. Photo by Gilbert.

Japan 2001. Ch. Taraglen Nautilus. Courtesy of McCarthy. Nautilus is a grandson of Spectre De La Rose (see pedigree charts on page 148).

In the Irish Setter, with the proportions of the shoulder blade and upper arm described above, the forelegs are set under the body, along the brisket. The pasterns are slightly sloping—at an angle sufficient to absorb the constant impact of the gallop without causing weakness. This slope of the pasterns, however, is only slight. The feet are rather small with arched toes and give the impression of being firm. Splayed feet and hare feet are undesirable, as they detract from the appearance of the dog and, more importantly, tend to cause discomfort during a long day's hunt. The entire front assembly is straight when viewed from the front, and must not give the appearance of too much width, although a pinched front also denotes weakness. Good bone is important, but should not be carried to excess. The front leg bones (radius and ulna) give an oval, rather than round, feel and appearance. Plenty of forechest and spring of rib are also important in a quality dog, but again must not be excessive. It is especially important that there is no impediment to the free flowing motion of the upper arm and foreleg. A barrel or widesprung chest will interfere with such movement, and also detract from the function of the animal.

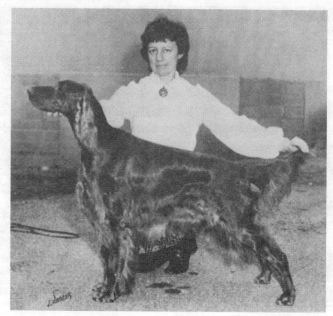

50 years of Irish Excellence.[xiv] *Photo by Shafer.*

Exaggerated streamlining often includes slabsidedness—a narrowing of the rib cage—a fault that reduces the size of the thoracic cavity, where lung room and the supply of oxygen during the hunt are all-important. Any length of the body should be the result of a longish back or rib cage, which includes the dorsal, but not lumbar, bones. With such features the loin or coupling can be moderately short and must be strong. A dog that is too short in the back and loin will compensate when moving, particularly at the trot, giving a crabbing or sidewinding gait. A dog that is too long will inevitably have a weak topline and will exhibit an inefficient gallop, which in turn results in lack of endurance. Since the loin is important in transferring power from the rear to the front of the dog, particularly at the gallop, the astute breeder and judge will assess its musculature. Superior muscling in the loin often produces a slightly perceived arch over this part of the body, and should not be penalized. The loin flows into the croup, which is very slightly sloped toward the set on of the tail. A croup that is too level does not allow the rear to get

*Photo courtesy of Dick and
Shirley Farrington.*

Photo by L. Stewart.

The Dog that commands attention.[xv]

Ch. Hartsbourne Sallyann of Tirvelda. (See pedigree charts on page 150)

sufficiently under the dog at the trot or gallop, and thus dimin-
ishes the thrust. The opposite extreme is a steep croup which
interferes with the ability of the rear to extend backwards and
provide power. The hindquarters drive the dog, and must be
wide and powerful with broad, well-developed thighs. Width
is vitally important since the gallop involves bringing the hind
legs well forward without interfering with the forelegs, which
at this stage of the gait are brought under the body. The hind
legs are long from the hip to the hock and are well-angulated,
but not so over-angulated as to destroy overall balance or
exhibit sickle hocks. The hocks are short and perpendicular to
the ground when standing still. Long hocks are incorrect in
this endurance dog, and also detract from the profile or silhouette of the Irish Setter. The angles in the dogs shown here are
correct. The rear assembly on the dog is powerful but not exaggerated. In an attempt to achieve a dramatic profile of an Irish
Setter in a posed position, breeders have too often selected for
show dogs with straight fronts and overangulated rears. The
topline of such specimens is spectacular at first glance but is
incorrect. The correct topline inclines slightly downwards. It
should be emphasized that the creation of this topline is not an
end in itself, but is a result of a long, well laid-back shoulder

Ch. Kinvarra Padraic Fagan with Robert A. Radcliffe. 1937.
Photo courtesy of the Radcliffe Family Collection.

The third generation. Chris and Robin.[xvi] 2001.

1998 Irish Setter at the Rocks. Photo by Bob Long.

and correct, balanced angulation in the rear, further enhanced
by a short strong hock. The tail is in proportion with the rest of
the dog, being strong at the root, not exaggerated, and extending not further than the hock joint. The tail carriage is most
important; it should be straight or nearly level with the back.
At the trot it is all-important both from a functional aspect, and
as an indicator of spirit and Irish Setter characteristic. A high
tail carriage ruins the appearance of the dog at a normal gait,
and should be penalized in the show ring. This fault can also
be the result of an incorrect rear assembly, particularly with a
sloping croup, and therefore would interfere with the dog's
stamina in the field.

Because the Irish Setter is an outgoing, happy dog, a constantly wagging tail is an indicator of the correct temperament.
At a show one's eye is drawn to the Irish Setters waiting to be
judged, because almost all of them will be attentive to their handlers and happily wagging their tail. Again, the enthusiasm for
activity and relationship with their master is characteristic of
the breed.

Ch. Taraglen Spellbinder with breeder, owner, handler Keith McCarthy. Australia. (see pedigree charts on page 151)

Coat, Color, and Texture

The coat of the Irish Setter provides the finishing touch to this glamorous breed. The rich chestnut or mahogany color, combined with substantial feathering, makes the Irish Setter one of the most beautiful of all dogs. Above all, the quality of the coat is important. Many specimens have excess coat which is of a wooly quality and easily forms unpleasant mats. The correct coat is short and fine on the head and forelegs, and elsewhere is of moderate length and flat. Feathering is long and silky on the ears, with a pleasing amount on the belly and brisket. On the tail there is a fringe of moderately long hair, which tapers to the tip. The amount of feathering carried by the modern-day show Irish Setter is certainly greater than was the case thirty years ago, yet it should be remembered by breeders, exhibitors, and judges alike that color and texture is always more important than length.

The Dog in Motion

All of the above-mentioned structural attributes must be translated into the gait of the Irish Setter. This is indeed a most difficult aspect of the breed to understand, but is of great importance in assessing the form of this wonderful gundog. The only means of assessing movement in the show ring is the trot. At the trot the gait is lively and graceful. Coming towards you, the front assembly—shoulders, upper arm, foreleg and foot should be traveling straightforward without deviation from a parallel relationship between the right and left. Excessive width at the elbows and shoulders, or excessive narrowing of the front will result in incorrect, wasted motion and takes away from the overall efficiency of the movement.

Rear action is more easily observed and understood. As with any aspect of the Irish Setter, no part of the movement should be exaggerated. There should be drive and extension of the second thigh and hock; the latter maintaining a perpendicular angle to the ground at moderate speed when viewed from

Irish Setter in the garden.

the rear, but as the speed increases tending to single track as viewed from behind. One consideration in assessing rear movement is that the Irish Setter in the field must be able to change direction readily, and therefore a wide gait with a foot fall farther apart than the distance between the hip bones is less than perfect. The tendency to exaggerate the standing profile of the breed has brought about an extremely undesirable prevalence of sickle hocks over recent years. Sickle hocks occur when the leg from the hockjoint to the ground slopes forward under the dog. In motion a dog with sickle hocks is limited in rear extension—a detriment to any galloping breed. Correct side gait is perhaps even more important to evaluate than the "down and back". There must be reach which results from the angles of the shoulder blade, upper arm and foreleg and their relative lengths. Eventually the foot should extend well forward at full extension, and at this point must be close to the ground in order to take advantage of the reach. A common fault is overreaching: here there is good extension, but at its furthest point the foot is several inches from the ground and is therefore incapable of providing efficient and powerful thrust. The fault can be described as "reaching for air". Additionally, many Irish Setters have the correct angles in the front but are restricted by a short upper arm and too wide a front. These dogs appear to be reaching, but careful observation will show that there is little extension beyond the brisket. These dogs have a busy scrambling gait, which is highly inefficient. Needless to say, a straight shoulder and upper arm will inevitably lead to a hackney gait. The strength and length of the neck are important in attaining correct movement and head carriage. The head is held high but forward of the withers and extends well forward as the speed of the dog increases. The tail in level carriage moves back and forth in harmony with the dog's motion and acts as a counterbalance to the forces involved in the gait. Nothing is more exciting and impressive than a well-conditioned, correctly balanced Irish Setter in full coat, being gaited on a lovely, smooth, green grass surface. A full understanding of the structure of the dog is fundamental to an evaluation of the trotting gait and will provide a means of assessing the movement of the dog at the gallop. This latter is the "business" gait of this type of gundog; it is not intended for a casual romp in the field chasing butterflies, but rather for an intense, high-energy exercise in the field, usually over a period of several hours. A dog of correct size and proportions and with the right attitude is capable of performing this function. The standard for the Irish Setter calls for a 27 inch dog and a 25 inch bitch (these measurements being made at the withers). The dedicated breeders who formulated this standard "got it right". The size is ideal for a dog intended to cover many miles in a day at a vigorous gallop, particularly in the open fields and moorland of Ireland. There is plenty of leg under the Irish Setter, and each stride covers ample ground without having to carry too much weight. A 29 inch dog might be useful in a selective breeding program but is not a correct specimen. Such a dog will exhibit energy and speed but will quickly tire. Thus size, proportions and overall balance are vitally important. Substance and strength without coarseness and weight characterizes the Irish Setter.

In attempting to capture the essence of the Irish Setter, one is hard pressed on the introductory statement in the present day American Kennel Club standard. *This is an active, aristocratic bird dog, rich red in color, substantial yet elegant in build. Standing over two feet tall at the shoulder, the dog has a straight fine glossy coat, longer on ears, chest tail and back of legs. Afield, the Irish Setter is a swift-moving hunter, at home, a sweet natured trainable companion. At their best the lines of the Irish Setter so satisfy in overall balance that artists (and many dedicated enthusiasts) have termed it the most beautiful of all dogs. The correct specimen always exhibits balance, whether standing or in motion. Each part of the dog flows and fits smoothly into its neighboring parts without calling attention to itself.* At work the Irish Setter is intent, energetic, efficient, and wildly enthusiastic about the task of locating game and assisting in its retrieval. This wonderful breed brings pleasure to many people throughout the world. The Irish Setter certainly deserves our nurturing, especially since it has such a long history as a hunting partner and companion.

Ch. Tirvelda Maidavale, 1966.
Ch. Legend of Varagond UDT x Ch. Tirvelda Sabrina.
Granddaughter of Ch. Tirvelda Michael Bryan
Great Granddaughter of Ch. Seaforth's Dark Rex, Thenderin Champagne,
Ch. Michael Bryan Duke of Sussex, Ch. Tirvelda Nutbrown Sherry,
and Ch. Hartsbourne Sallyann of Tirvelda.

Irish Setter Pedigrees

In the hands of skilled and knowledgeable breeders, both line breeding and outcrossing can be successful. Two excellent examples come from two influential kennels of the 1950-1980 period; these are the Tirvelda and Thenderin Kennels. The early Thenderin pedigrees contain many outcrosses, but later this was followed by much closer linebreeding. The early outcrosses were carried out with a knowledge of structure and type to bring top quality into the breeding program. The later linebreeding provided the distinctive Thenderin type with good front and rear angles that were well-matched, and with strong level toplines. One of the most influential products William Muldoon, a top-winning dog who garnered the best of breed honors at the second Irish Setter National Specialty. William Muldoon in turn produced Ch. Kilgary Dungannon and Ch. Kimberlin O'Killea of Top'O, both top winners and producers.

Ted Eldredge's Tirvelda Kennel made a fresh start in its breeding program in the late 1950's with the importation from England, of the lovely bitch, Ch. Hartsbourne Sallyann of Tirvelda. A product of the first litter bred by Tirvelda was the influential Ch. Kinvarra Kermit who in turn sired Ch. Kinvarra Portia, the foundation bitch of Thenderin. Sallyann was bred first to Ch. Kinvarra Malone to produce the great dam, Ch. Tirvelda Nutbrown Sherry. Sherry when bred to the midwestern dog, Ch. Michael Bryan Duke of Sussex had a litter of great prominence, and out of 12 puppies, 11 finished their championship. Males from this litter included Ch. Tirvelda Michaelson, Ch. Tirvelda Nor'wester and Ch. Tirvelda Earl of Harewood all of whom had a great influence on the breed. Thus, it was via the outcross of the imported English bitch followed by skillful line breeding that this whole line developed. Ted Eldredge was never afraid to outcross and was very successful, however, he had an in-depth knowledge of the breed and always bred correct type to correct type. He was able to achieve the same balance of well-angled fronts and rears that characterized the Thenderin Irish Setters. One Tirvelda bitch who typified the kennel was the lovely Ch. Tirvelda Maidavale. Maida's dam, Ch. Tirvelda Sabrina, was out of Sherry's litter sister by one of the 11 champions produced in the record-breaking litter. The sire of Maida was a Californian dog and so Maida was a true outcross. Ted Eldredge produced the same type of Irish Setter whether via outcross breeding or linebreeding. Later dogs that owed much to Tirvelda were Ch. McCamon Marquis and Ch. Tirvelda Distant Drummer both of whom were much more tightly bred to the Tirvelda line than their earlier predecessors.

Several other major kennels of the same vintage as Thenderin and Tirvelda were also highly influential. Lucy Jane Myers' Draherin made many contributions to the breed. The foundation of Draherin Auburn Artistry who was sired by the Southern Californian dog, Ch. Innisfail Color Scheme, became an important part of the Draherin breeding program. Auburn Artistry was a real "stallion" of a dog with excellent conformation. His influence is with us today particularly through his son, Ch. Draherin County Leitrim. The most important Draherin sire was a dog acquired from another great kennel, Shannon. This dog was Ch. Shannon's Erin who for a time was "neck and neck" with Ch. Tirvelda Michaelson for top honors as a sire of champions. Erin was a stylish medium-sized dog who produced some wonderful dogs; he was also a top show dog winning several best-in-show awards and twice won best-of-breed at the Westminster Kennel Club show.

The Southern California influence on the breed was not confined to Thenderin. Other great kennels emerged, such as Webline. By far the most important dog in the Webline breeding program was the foundation sire, Ch. Innisfail Color Scheme. This dog, bred by the Jeromes, was sired by the great Ch. Seaforth's Dark Rex out of Thenderin Champagne. What followed was a strong line of highly successful show dogs guided in their careers by the founder of Webline, Dick Webb.

Many other kennels of significance were contemporaries of those mentioned above including Varagon, Knockross, Argo Lane, and Muckamoor.

In Australia and New Zealand there are Irish Setters of quality. A third pedigree is included here as a paradigm of breeding practice. Taraglen is a combination of superior Australian lines (originally from England) with recent outcrosses to lines from the United States. Ch. Taraglen Jenufa, the challenge winning bitch at the Melbourne, Specialty 1982, delights the memory.

Irish Setter Pedigree

Am. & Can. Ch. Michael Bryan Duke of Sussex
Whelped 1955

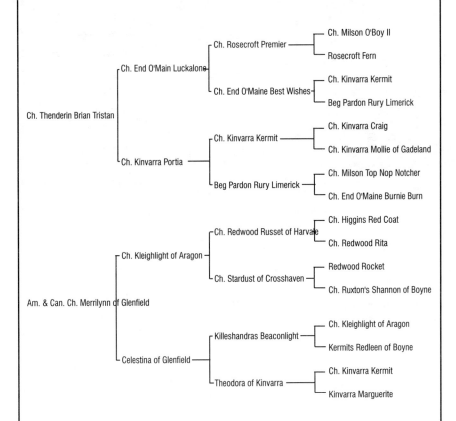

Irish Setter Pedigree

Ch. Tirvelda Nutbrown Sherry
Whelped 1960

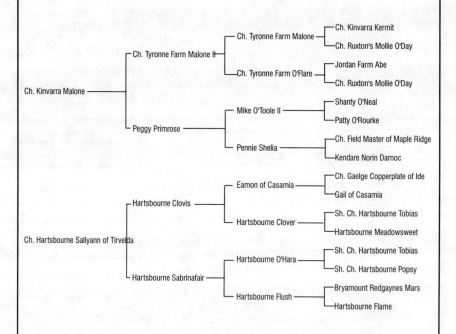

Ch. Kinvarra Malone
- Ch. Tyronne Farm Malone II
  - Ch. Tyronne Farm Malone
    - Ch. Kinvarra Kermit
    - Ch. Ruxton's Mollie O'Day
  - Ch. Tyronne Farm O'Flare
    - Jordan Farm Abe
    - Ch. Ruxton's Mollie O'Day
- Peggy Primrose
  - Mike O'Toole II
    - Shanty O'Neal
    - Patty O'Rourke
  - Pennie Shelia
    - Ch. Field Master of Maple Ridge
    - Kendare Norin Darnoc

Ch. Hartsbourne Sallyann of Tirvelda
- Hartsbourne Clovis
  - Eamon of Casamia
    - Ch. Gaelge Copperplate of Ide
    - Gail of Casamia
  - Hartsbourne Clover
    - Sh. Ch. Hartsbourne Tobias
    - Hartsbourne Meadowsweet
- Hartsbourne Sabrinafair
  - Hartsbourne O'Hara
    - Sh. Ch. Hartsbourne Tobias
    - Sh. Ch. Hartsbourne Popsy
  - Hartsbourne Flush
    - Bryamount Redgaynes Mars
    - Hartsbourne Flame

Irish Setter Pedigree

Ch. Taraglen Tudor Rose
Whelped March 8, 1995

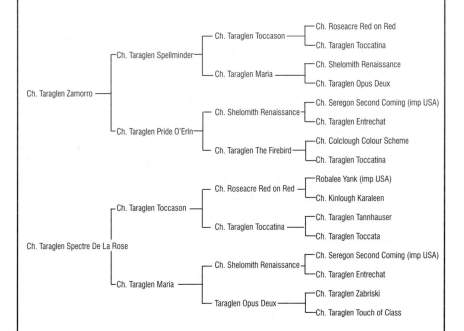

Note: On Ch. Taraglen Tudor Rose's pedigree some further
information about animals appearing in the 5th generation column

Ch. Colclough Colour Scheme and Ch. Roseacre Red on Red are half-brothers
Ch. Taraglen Touch of Class and Ch. Taraglen Entrechat are litter sisters

Endnotes

1   Denlinger, M.G., *The Complete Irish Setter*, Denlinger's, Washington D.C. 1949.

2   Caius, Johannes (In Tuck, Davis, 1951) physician to Edward VI, Queen Mary and Elizabeth I. The founder of Caius (Key's) College in Cambridge.

3   *Irish Setters* by Frederick J. Haycock. (Color Plate 22).

4   Eldredge, E.I. and Vanacore, C., *The New Complete Irish Setter*, Howell Book House Inc. New York, 1983, (Page 16).

Photo Endnotes

i.   May this photo serve to remind us of the significant contributions to all setters and the sport of dogs by Tom Tobin pictured here with Am., Can., & Mex., Ch. Rendition Chantilly Lace.

ii.   Ch. Quailmoor Jump N Jack Flash owned by Norma Hamilton.

iii. Generations of Irish at Rendition.

iv.   Emily Bisso—a second generation Irish owner.

v.   Paula McAteer with Redstar.

vi.   Ch. Thenderin Legacy.

vii. Left to Right: WB Laurel Ridge Bombshell, RB Knights Croft Encore.

viii. Ch. Thenderin Wind Ruler.

ix.   Ch. End O'Maine McCabe owned by Orrin Evans.

x.   Ch. Seaforth's Dark Rex.

xi.   Ch. Draherin King's Ransom.

xii. Claudia Weninger with Thenderin Vixon.

xiii. Ch. Seaforth's Dark Rex owned by Orrin Evans.

xiv. Breeder, owner, handler, and judge, Claire Andrews of Rhode Island with her top producing bitch Ch. Kimberlin Cara.

xv   Ch. Thenderin Brian Tristan. Tristan was Best American Bred in Show at Westminster.

xvi. Chris is the grandson of Robert A. Radcliffe and is the owner and handler of Irish Setters.

6 Art and the Setter Type

by Dennis J. Sporre

Introduction

𝒯he purpose of this chapter is to describe and evaluate individual and collective images of the setter type in visual art. In pursuing that purpose we will break little new ground. That is to say, this chapter is not an exhaustive study; its length prohibits that. Nor is it an attempt to define the existence of established setter types in time by finding the very first appearance of one or another of the setters in art. Rather, this study assumes that the histories of the breeds, as set forth in their official AKC descriptions, are correct. Nonetheless, in the course of our examination we will find some arguably interesting twists on those assumptions. As previously stated, however, none of this is new. Ultimately, the goal of this chapter is to provide information which can enhance our understanding of images of the Irish, Gordon, English, and Red and White setters wherever in art we find them. In order successfully to meet that goal, we must understand not only when and how the setter appears in art, but also what that appearance means in the larger context of art itself.

Consequently, this chapter has a two-part organization. The first part explains a bit about the concerns, purposes, and functions of art, and the nature of artistic style. This assists in understanding how to view representations of the setter type examined in the second part of the chapter. The second part of the chapter consists of analyses of works of art over several centuries. Included are references to other works of art as well as URLs, or internet addresses, at which more works can be viewed. With regard to URLs, however, a warning is necessary. First, things change. A web site active when this book went to press may no longer exist. Second, an initial attempt to link to a site may prove unsuccessful: "Unable to connect to remote host." A rule of thumb is to try to connect to the site three successive times before trying another URL. Be careful to type the URL exactly. Any incorrect character will cause the connection to fail (capital letters matter).

Some Basics About Art

Critically examining the appearance of setters in art requires a basic comprehension of art itself. This chapter does not intend to be about art appreciation. Nevertheless, familiarity with the art environment that produced setter representations can be quite helpful. Thus, we begin with a few comments about the concerns, purposes, and functions of art. That is followed by comments about artistic style, which gives us a framework for interpreting both the way setters are depicted and what we can learn from that depiction about the breeds themselves.

Throughout history, art has typically concerned four things: creativity, aesthetic communication, symbols, and "fine art" and "applied art". Art has always involved creativity—that is, bringing forth new forces and forms. How this functions is subject to debate, but it is clear that humankind is impelled to transform chaos, formlessness, vagueness, and the unknown into form, design, inventions, and ideas. Creativity underlies our existence. It allows scientists to intuit that there is a possible path to a cure for cancer or to invent a computer. Similar processes allow artists to find new ways to express ideas in which creative action, thought, material, and technique combine in a medium such as painting to create something that evokes human experience—specifically, a response to the artwork. The artists who created pictures that include setters intended to say something about the dog. Sometimes the comments are incidental and sometimes they are primary, but always they are intentional.

And thus our second point: art involves communication, which is by nature a humanizing experience. Artists need other people with whom they can share their perceptions, and when artworks and humans interact, many possibilities exist. Interaction may be casual and fleeting, as in the first meeting of two people when one or both are not at all interested in the other. An artist may not have much to say, or may not say it very well; a poorly conceived and executed painting probably will not excite a viewer. If, on the other hand, the viewer is self-absorbed, distracted, unaware, has rigid preconceptions not met by the painting, or is otherwise preoccupied so as not to perceive what the artwork offers, then at least part of the artistic experience fizzles. Yet under the best of conditions a profoundly exciting and meaningful experience may occur: the painting may treat a significant subject in a unique manner, the painter's skill in manipulating the medium may be excellent, and the viewer may be receptive. Or the interaction may fall somewhere between these two extremes. For example, a photographically accurate, illustrative, but artistically mundane portrait of a setter may provoke profound emotional response in the dog's owner, but only a "ho-hum" response in someone else. In any case, the experience is a human one, and that is fundamental to art.

Throughout history, artistic communication has involved *aesthetics.* Aesthetics is the study of the nature of beauty and of art, and comprises one of the five classical fields of philosophical inquiry—along with epistemology (the nature and origin of knowledge), ethics (the general nature of morals and of the specific moral choices to be made by the individual in relationship with others), logic (the principles of reasoning), and metaphysics (the nature of first principles and problems of ultimate reality). The term "aesthetics" (from the Greek for "sense perception") was coined by German philosopher Alexander Baumgarten in the mid-18th century, but interest in what constitutes the beautiful and in the relationship between art and nature goes back at least to the ancient Greeks. Both Plato and Aristotle saw art as *imitation,* and beauty as the expression of a universal quality. To the Greeks the concept of "art" embraced all handcrafts, and the rules of symmetry, proportion, and unity applied equally to weaving and pottery, poetry and sculpture. These principles persist to the present in perceiving works of art, and we shall see them again, momentarily, in approaching setters in art.

In the late 18th century, the philosopher Immanuel Kant revolutionized aesthetics in his *Critique of Judgment* (1790) by viewing aesthetic appreciation not simply as the perception of intrinsic beauty, but as involving a judgment—subjective, but informed. Since Kant, the primary focus of aesthetics has shifted from the consideration of beauty per se to the nature of the artist, the role of art, and the relationship between the viewer and the work of art. General aesthetics, thus, can play a fundamental role in interpreting the appearance of a setter in a work of art.

Third, art is concerned with symbols, that is, with physical manifestations that represent something else. Often the physical symbol represents an abstract idea or an intangible relationship: a wedding ring, for example, can symbolize unending fidelity and love. Symbols differ from signs, which indicate a fact or condition. Signs are what they denote. Symbols carry deeper, wider, and richer meanings. By employing symbols to communicate, artworks can project thoughts and feelings that go well beyond the surface meaning of the work and offer glimpses of the human condition that cannot be adequately evoked in any other manner. We can see how symbols make artworks into doorways leading to enriched meaning when we consider the appearance of a dog in a painting. From earliest times the dog has symbolized, among other things, marital faith. When we find a dog in a family portrait, especially prior to the twentieth century, the artist's intention probably is more concerned with the nature of interpersonal relations than with the dog. That is to say, the presence of the dog indicates not only common ownership of the animal but, more important, the stability and serenity of the family itself.

Fourth, a basic understanding of art involves knowing the difference between "fine art" and "applied art." The "fine arts"—generally meaning painting, sculpture, and architecture—are prized for their purely aesthetic qualities. During the Renaissance (approximately 1400-1600), these arts rose to superior status because Renaissance values prized individual expression and unique aesthetic interpretations of ideas. The term "applied art" sometimes includes architecture but generally refers to art forms that have a primarily decorative rather than expressive or emotional purpose. The decorative arts include handicrafts by skilled artisans, such as ornamental work in metal, stone, wood, and glass as well as textiles, pottery, and bookbinding. The term may also encompass furniture and interior design. In addition, personal objects such as jewelry, weaponry, tools, and costumes often fall under the heading of the decorative arts. The term, which first appeared in 1791, may even extend to some mechanical appliances and other products of industrial design. Such decorative arts as weaving, basketry, or pottery, are also commonly referred to as "crafts" or "handicrafts," but the definition of the terms here becomes somewhat arbitrary and without sharp distinction. As will be noted later, the appearance of a setter in a work of fine art may have different implications than the appearance of a setter in a work of craft.

We have just examined what art concerns. We must now understand art's purposes and functions. In the former case we are dealing with its aims, in the latter with how those aims are realized. Essentially, art does four things: It provides a record; it gives visible form to feelings; it reveals metaphysical or spiritual truths; and it helps people see the world in new or innovative ways. A work of art can do any or all of these. They are not mutually exclusive.

Until the invention of the camera in the 19th century, one of art's principal purposes was to enact a record of the world. We will see this clearly in the earliest of our examples of setters in art. Art can also give visible form to feelings. Perhaps the most explicit example of this aspect of art comes in the Expressionist style of the early twentieth century. Here the artist' emotional response to his subject matter plays a primary role in the work. Feelings find expression in works of art through technique—for example, brushstroke—and through color, both of which have long associations with emotional content. Art can also aim at the revelation of metaphysical or spiritual truths. Think for example of the great Gothic cathedrals of Europe, whose light and space perfectly embodied medieval spirituality. The rising line of the cathedral reaches, ultimately, to the point of the spire, which symbolizes the release of earthly space into the unknown space of heaven. The relevance of this characteristic comes clear in reference to an early tapestry, discussed below, that may or may not accurately represent a setter. Finally, most art, if well executed, can assist us in seeing the world around us in new and surprising ways. Certainly one example would be Duchamp's *Nude Descending a Stair Case*.

In addition to its purposes art has a number of characteristic functions: it can furnish enjoyment, serve as a political or social weapon, and provide artifacts. One is no more important than the others. Nor, again, are they mutually exclusive; one artwork may perform many functions. Nor are the three just mentioned the only ones. Rather, they serve as indicators of how art has served in the past and can act in the present. The last of these, art as a product of a particular time and place, is especially relevant to our concerns, for extant works of art serve to help us understand how setter type has developed over time.

Finally, the manner in which artists express themselves constitutes their style. Style is tantamount to the personality of an artwork. Style is that body of characteristics that identifies an artwork with an individual, a historical period, a nation, or a school such as realism, expressionism, or cubism. Understanding the style of any artwork entails determining how the artist has employed the technical and expressive potential of a medium. This is particularly important in attempting to determine the accuracy of the setter type in works of art, because not all styles pursue lifelikeness as a priority. Thus, the appearance of a "setter" in one style may be a faithful representation of what the dog really looked like. In another style, appearance and verisimilitude may have little in common.

The Setter in Art

This grounding in art fundamentals prepares us to examine some representations of setters and draw a few conclusions. The first example, and certainly a very early one, is the Devonshire Hunting Tapestry (c. 1400's CE) from the Victoria and Albert Museum in London, England. Here, the dog (Color Plate 1) is identified as a Setting Spaniel. No less an authority than C. Bede Maxwell asserts in her book, *The Truth About Sporting Dogs*, that "setter shape is clearly identifiable" in this representation. As Mrs. Maxwell points out, the coat pattern and feathering are of interest. What we cannot determine from this work of craft is the actual size of the dog. The lack of determinable scale is not the only factor that bars us from drawing firm conclusions. For example, the tapestry is dated in very general terms: "circa 1400s." Although the 1400s (in Italian, *quattrocento*) represent the beginnings of the Renaissance, with its lifelike depictions, the style of the tapestry is more characteristic of late Gothic, an earlier, medieval style in which spirituality, exaggeration, and emotion are primary foci. These elements are evident in the picture's elongation of forms and lack of rational perspective. In other words, the presentation abounds in exaggeration. Forgetting about the dog for a moment and concentrating on the other forms leads to the conclusion that this tapestry does not offer a slice of life so much as an idealized conception of components arranged for design purposes. There is, nonetheless, pictorial record in this tapestry. Costume and hairstyle, for example, reasonably represent the silhouette and textures of the period, but, again, not in a fully lifelike manner. As a result, pulling the dog out of its context yields little certainty about its scale, shape, or color, and, hence, its representation of the setter type. Most likely, the tapestry is a stylized conception of a dog rather than a portrait of any dog in particular. As the Italian *vedutistas* of the eighteenth century proved, even those things in paintings that purport to be real scenes of real places are often altered to suit the artist's purposes. Thus, even though our analysis may not provide a definitive conclusion, the informed application of art history and principles will yield the most accurate perception possible.

Perhaps one of the most interesting depictions of what is clearly the modern day Irish Setter type appears in a portrait by Anthony Van Dyck (1599-1641) entitled *The Fourth Earl of Pembroke and Family* (Color Plate 3). It raises a number of notable issues. To begin, Van Dyck was court painter to the English King Charles I and one of several Dutch painters imported to England for the specific purpose of painting royal, aristocratic, and bourgeois portraits. It would take another century for England to produce her own rather impressive stable of portrait and landscape artists, among whom Gainsborough and Constable are exemplary. Van Dyck was not above manipulating a painting's environment to his patron's advantage (he regularly portrayed the king truthfully and yet as a quietly imposing figure, taller even than his horse, for example). Still nothing in the portrait of the Pembroke family suggests that he has doctored the background in such a way as to alter the appearance of the dog.

This painting reflects the intellectual, spiritual, and social energy manifested by Europe in the seventeenth century. It typifies the Baroque, a style often characterized by an ornate opulence and emotional appeal, and widely valued by those intent to secure or advance their reputation or status. Most important, since paintings in the baroque style are typically true to life, we can generally trust their depictions. The date of the painting, 1634, places it very near the commonly agreed upon appearance of the Irish Setter as a breed type: the official histories date the Irish to the early seventeenth century. The dog in this portrait painting has all the qualities of the modern Irish Setter. Its color is a rich mahogany, and its size is clearly in the vicinity of twenty-seven or so inches. The coat would do any modern show setter proud, and, although the head is ever so slightly down-faced, the planes are nearly parallel, the stop is distinct, the muzzle square with no throatiness, the skull lean, and the ears long and set low. The silhouette is distinctly Irish. In other words, in 1634, Van Dyck faithfully pictured was in all regards a modern Irish Setter.

By the eighteenth century, painting had moved from the opulent and emotional baroque style to a new approach called "genre." Paintings in this style were imbued with interest in the mundane. In their gentle, unobtrusive contemplation of the world, such common items as cooking pots, ladles, pitchers, bottles, corks, and slabs of meat were invested with significance. Richness of texture and color combined with sensitive composition and the use of *chiaroscuro* (highlight and shadow) make these humble items somehow noble. Typically, there is pure poetry in the genre artist's brush. We are subtly urged to see beyond the surface impression of the objects themselves into a deeper reality. Although genre art features still life, artists such as Sir Joshua Reynolds (1723-92) and Thomas Gainsborough (1727-88) combined portraiture and genre scenes into a "family picture" type of painting that became very popular by the end of the eighteenth century. In contrast with the aristocratic subjects of the Baroque period, these works often depicted middle-class patrons who dressed up as peasants or farmers in staged scenes of rural life.

Yet in spite of its inclination to realistic portraiture, genre painting is a far from perfect source of understanding of dogs in general and setters in particular. Until the nineteenth century, dogs, although often depicted, were usually ancillary subjects and rarely identified as to breed. For that reason, we can hold up any number of works of art and argue about whether this or that one actually portrays an English, Irish, Gordon, or Red and White Setter. A pair of examples by Thomas Gainsborough and George Romney make the point. In Gainsborough's (1787) *The Marsham Children* (Color Plate 2) our eye is drawn to the small white and lemon dog in the lower left corner. Although its silhouette is similar to the setter dog in Sir Nathaniel Bacon's "*Self portrait*" and Stephen Slaughter's "*Windham Quin*"[1] it only suggests more setter than spaniel. In George Romneys (1777) *Clavering Children*[2] we see the spaniel colors in red and white and black and tan that have also been known since the earliest times in the setters. Further, the long shallow-flewed muzzle, the alert ear carriage, and the dark nose on the white dog which stands at least six inches taller may depict an early setter-perhaps a Red and White.

As an age wracked by social, political, and cultural transitions, the nineteenth century exhibits astounding change and diversity in art, as well as in literature, politics, and technology. In short, much of western society was undergoing a sea change of hitherto unimaginable proportions. Culturally, the first half of the century was dominated by the Romantic movement. This reaction against eighteenth century classicism and formality was marked by an emphasis on subjective experience, personal freedom, and the exaltation of nature—especially its wild and extreme forms. Hence the artist is a truly unique lens or filter through which reality is to be viewed anew.

Yet with mid-century came the full flowering of the Victorian Era, an often staid and moralistic counter-reaction which in the world of painting gave rise to realism and, near the end of the century, impressionism and post-impressionism, with all three emphasizing different viewpoints and approaches.

But at least as concerns the depictions of setters, things become clearer. The Victorian love of animals is legendary, and owning bizarre, wild, and exotic pets became the rage, a development characteristic of the Romantic tendency and outlook. In the jubilee year of 1887, thousands of prisoners all over the British Empire were released. The only criminals not released were those convicted of cruelty to animals, which Queen Victoria regarded as "one of the worst traits of human nature." In this period dogs became a regular, central focus of painters, and they were often anthropomorphized (that is, given human attributes).

Early in the 19th century, the English painter Philip Reinagle (1749-1833) created numerous dog paintings, many of which have been turned into popular contemporary prints and posters. In his portrait of an English Setter,1804 (Color Plate 6) the dog assumes the central focus in its natural hunting environment. Stylistically, the work has several interesting aspects. The foreground exhibits the detailed realism and smooth brush stroke of the age, and typical of thegenre subjects, mentioned earlier, that emerged in the mid-18th century in such artists as Jean-Baptiste-Siméon Chardin (1699-1779). The background fades into a more painterly approach with spontaneous brush-work and atmospherics. The setter, however, stands center stage and details of color, musculature, coat, and structure have been rendered flawlessly right down to the nicely arched toes and strong pasterns. Reinagle's use of color contrast and careful application of light and shadow (*chiaroscuro*) bring the dog into position not only as the central focus of the painting, but also as its anchoring compositional device. In a tactic vaguely reminiscent of Rembrandt's famous painting *The Night Watch*, Reinagle invents his light source rather than relying on natural illumination. Clearly the front two-thirds of the dog could not be highlighted as Reinagle indicates. He is creating an emotional effect by focusing the viewer's attention on what he wishes to emphasize—that is, the head and forequarters of the dog intent on its job. Note, though, that the man, although a seemingly peripheral background figure, looms above the dog, suggesting in hierarchical fashion the ever-present dominance of the master.

Perhaps the foremost dog specialist of mid-19th century painting was Sir Edwin Henry Landseer (1802-73). Fortunately for dog lovers, Sir Edwin regularly took the trouble to identify the breed he portrayed. Most of Landseer's pictures were well known from excellent engravings of them by his elder brother Thomas. Two examples can be seen on line.[3] In the first example, *Pointer and Setter* the two dogs are after a rabbit with the setter in traditional point position showing a magnificent profile of head, the obvious peak of the shoulders and the taught extension of the horizontal tail. In the second Landseer example, *A Setter Dog*, the setter is clearly an Irish, with all of the modern characteristics present. What is notable, as suggested earlier, is the Victorian interest in the dog as a primary subject. This work is not "about" anything other than the setter pictured. As a consequence, the subject is seen in its own right as worthy of the value bestowed on it by the artist's interest and investiture. The setter is not posed nor involved in any activity that could be denoted as "human-inspired." At rest and yet gently alert, the dog exhibits nobility and serenity. What

Landseer does in this work is to raise the setter to a level of honor and distinction, akin to the sanctification of nature typical of the Romantic Age. The Tate Gallery in London, England[4] has additional works by Landseer in which similar ennobling of dogs is evident.

As if to prove that new art never replaces old in the way that new science replaces old science, by the late 19th century many artists had returned dogs to a supporting role in contemporary portraiture. The American realist painter Thomas Eakins puts the family dog comfortably at home in a portrait of his wife *The Artist's Wife and his Setter Dog;* undated (Color Plate 7). The setter dog referenced in the title is an Irish, as evidenced by the rust-colored coat. The central focus, however, is Eakin's wife, Susan Macdowell Eakins. The artist's use of strong color contrast to draw the eye to his wife makes this clear. The setter ("his" not "their") barely emerges from the oriental carpet, whose color is close to the dog's. Even if not the central focus, however, the dog does provide a central compositional function as the stabilizing base of the triangle around which Eakins organizes his painting. The wife's posture is reminiscent of James Whistler's famous portrait of his mother. How subtle or ironic Eakins might have been in this family portrait one can only guess. The positioning of the burly, resting dog at the base of the compositional triangle, soaking up the warm reds of the carpet, in contrast with the fussy textures and cool blues of the wife's dress does merit speculation.

In the pre-war years of the twentieth century we find a fascinating group portrait of English Setters in German painter Edmund Henry Osthaus's *Seven English Setters*[5] (Color Plate 8). The purpose of Osthaus's work is to glorify sporting dogs, and his work was particularly admired by such wealthy American families as the Vanderbilts and the Morgans. Plebian in technique, the painting nonetheless exhibits some noteworthy elements. It is a romantic and staged assembly in the guise of an informal moment. The loose brushwork lends an air of spontaneity *à la* the impressionists. Osthaus plays with the composition, lining up the leading edge of the setters along the diagonal axis of the painting and juxtaposing the soft texture of fur and the curvilinear shapes of the dogs with the hard surface and rectilinear elements of the table and lattice. This arrangement puts motion into an otherwise placid, almost sleepy arrangement, but leaves the work unbalanced with no apparent logic to its escape from the frame, especially on the left margin. Notwithstanding, the artist is intent on presenting the typical features of the breed. The varieties of coloring come forth, as do qualities of eye placement, expression, muzzle, ear set, skull, feet, bone density, shoulder layback, and so on. In a carefully calculated statement, the docile personality of the English Setter emerges in the laid back slumber of one of the confreres amid the tension of the group pose.

It has been noted that setters appear frequently in portraiture and often as models for study, yet they seem most comfortable on canvas in the realm of their human masters, engaging in their fundamental purpose: hunting. G. Muss-Arnolt (1858-1927) exhibits a style that has become almost stereotypical of twentieth-century dog art. In *English Setter, Gordon Setter, and Pointer* (Color Plate 9) we discover the breeds, fully distinguished modern types, engaged in the hunt. Muss-Arnolt was a highly respected dog show judge, and his works, according to the American Kennel Club, in whose collection this painting hangs, are accurate reflections of the *desired conformations*. In artistic terms, then, Muss-Arnolt has moved from accurate depiction of specific animals into an idealized depiction of a type. This raises the question of whether one should view his paintings as reflecting the actual dogs of the era or his personal conception of what the dogs *ought* to be. In a sense, we seem to have come full circle from our fifteenth-century starting point wherein on the basis of style we questioned the reliability of the artistic rendering in helping us discern the actual state of the breed reflected in the art.

Color Plate References

1. Devonshire Hunting Tapestry, *Falconry Tapestry*
2. Van Dyck, *The Fourth Earl of Pembroke and Family*
3. Gainsborough, *The Marsham Children*
4. Reinagle, *Sportsmen with Setter and Pheasant*
5. Eakins, *The Artist's Wife and His Setter Dog*
6. Osthaus, *Seven English Setters*
7. Muss-Arnolt, *English Setter, Gordon Setter, and Pointer*

Endnotes

1   Leighton-Boyce, Gilbert, 1985.

2   http://www.huntington.org/ArtDiv/ClaveringPict.html

3   http://search.famsf.org/4d.acgi$Record?5644&=list&=21&=edw
     in&=And&=24&=0&=keywords&=Yes&=landseer%20&=&=&=
     Yes&=&=f

4   www.tate.org.uk

5   Edmund Henry Osthaus painted *Seven English Setters* in the year
     1911.

Color Plate Endnotes

Plates 1, 2, 3, 6, 7, 8, 9

Please refer to discussion of these paintings by Dennis Sporre in Chapter 6, "Art and the Setter Type".

Plate 4

This illustration by Edwards for his book on British dogs takes on new meaning when presented in color. The two dogs on the right are setters in head type, tails, and color (one white with red patches and the other a dark red self colored dog) while the two dogs on the left are the long, low spaniel with long, heavily coated ears, docked tails, wide short heads, and abundant coats.

Plate 5

Edwards' illustration of setters shows one of the earliest examples of the diverse colors and perhaps even the subtle diversity of work pattern. The beautiful mahogany setter with the white blaze on the skull and muzzle stands tall in a backing position while the white setter is in a lying position (just as Caius describes) and the black and tan setter is in a set position with tail straight and low. The yellow eyes that offend today's viewer were common in most dog breeds of that time.

Plate 8

Edmund Henry Osthaus, a German sportsman and artist came to the United States in 1880 and became famous for his paintings of setters and pointers. An avid hunter, field trial competitor and judge he maintained a kennel of setters for many years.

Plate 10

This painting by Morland has been claimed by every breed that even remotely resembles this red and white hunting dog. Comparing the type to the setters of the same period painted by Edwards in Plate 8 it is clear that this is a setter. When compared to the paintings that are documented as Irish Red and White Setters in the Brigden book, these dogs are the same in color and type.

Plate 14

C.C. Hendee was a well known painter of sporting dogs in the United States. He was commissioned by Dr. A.A. Mitten, of Happy Valley Kennels to paint his favorite setters. This is one of a set of three English Setter portraits given by Mitten to famous judge Teddy Hayes who had been the groomer at Happy Valley in the 1920's and early 30's when Blue Dan was a top winning dog. Mrs. Hayes presented the collection to the author in New York in 1964.

Plate 26

Ch. Tirvelda Queen Mab. Courtesy of the Tirvelda Collection.

Color Plate 1

15th Century
FALCONRY TAPESTRY *of the*
Devonshire Hunting Collection
(Permission from the Victoria
and Albert Museum, London)

The Falconry Tapestry, woven at
Tournai, Flanders and dated by
authorities at fifteenth century,
shows the sport of hunting with
falcons and dogs. The scene
includes a woman in the most
elegant hunting dress and hat
with a falconer who is preparing
to release his bird toward flying
ducks. The dog is small, light
colored, muscular, feathered like
a setter, and ready to work for its
master. This must also serve to
delight the sportswomen in setters today who have become an essential part
of the field training with all four setter breeds.

Color Plate 2

1787
Thomas Gainsborough
THE MARSHAM
CHILDREN
(Permission from
the Staaliche Museen
zu Berlin)

Color Plate 3

1634 Anthony Van Dyck
Detail from THE FOURTH EARL OF PEMBROKE AND FAMILY
(From the private collection of The Earl of Pembroke, Wilton House, Salisbury, U.K.)

THE SPANIEL.

London Pub. by Syd. Edwards. Jan. 1st 1801.

Color Plate 4

1801
Sydenham Teast Edwards
THE SPANIEL

(From Cynographia Britannica, London. Courtesy of Robert and Marsha Brown)

Syd. Edwards. Sculp.

THE SETTER

Color Plate 5

1805
Sydenham Teast Edwards
THE SETTER

(From Cynographia Britannica, London. Courtesy of Robert and Marsha Brown)

Color Plate 6

1804 Philip Reinagle R.A.
SPORTSMEN WITH SETTER AND PHEASANT *from the Scott print "Setter"*
(American Kennel Club Collection)

Color Plate 7

19th Century
Thomas Eakins
THE ARTIST'S WIFE
AND SETTER DOG

*(The Metropolitan
Museum of Art, Fletcher
Fund, 1923. [23.139]
Photograph © 1993
The Metropolitan
Museum of Art)*

Color Plate 8

1911 Edmund Henry Osthaus
SEVEN ENGLISH SETTERS
(American Kennel Club Collection)

Color Plate 9

19th Century G. Muss-Arnolt
ENGLISH SETTER, GORDON SETTER, AND POINTER
(American Kennel Club Collection)

Color Plate 10

1806 George Morland
The Ward mezzotint SETTERS
(From the private collection of John and Jackie Kessler)

Color Plate 11

1855
Richard Ansdell
THE SCOTTISH
GAMEKEEPER
*(Permission from
Clive Rex Alexander)*

Color Plate 12

1920 R. Ward Binks
RUFFLYN CAPRICE
(From the private collection of
Anne Savory Bolus)

Color Plate 13

2000 ENGLISH SETTER
HEAD STUDY BITCH

Color Plate 14

1929 C. C. Hendee
CHAMPION BLUE DAN OF HAPPY VALLEY
(From the Robert and Marsha Brown Collection)

Color Plate 15

1995 English Setter Tri-Color Male
(Photo by Jannard)

Color Plate 16

1983
English Setter Blue Belton Bitch
(Photo by Ashby)

Color Plate 17

1989
English Setter Orange Belton Male
(Photo by Gourlay)

Color Plate 18

19th Century John M. Tracy
BOB
(American Kennel Club Collection)

Color Plate 19

1985
Gordon Setters with an English Setter, and an Irish Setter
(Photo by Dawn Ferguson, New South Wales, Australia)

Color Plate 20

1775 George Stubbs
Detail from Sportsmen at Rest
(Permission from the National Gallery of Ireland, Dublin)

Color Plate 21

19th Century S. J. E. Jones
Two Sportsmen and Setters in the Field
(American Kennel Club Collection)

Color Plate 22

1993 Frederick J. Haycock
IRISH SETTERS
(From the private collection of John Savory)

Color Plate 23

Irish Setter Head Study Male

Color Plate 24

Irish Setter Head Study Bitch

7 | The Breed Standards

by Peter A. Frost

From their inception breed standards were intended by their authors to provide a blueprint of the breed for the use of both breeders and judges. They were an ideal that breeders must strive to maintain so that the breed might continue in its purest form regardless of location as well as a guide to be used when evaluating their stock or selecting puppies. For judges they were to provide the criteria to use when assessing exhibits in the show ring. Since judges' decisions influence breeders and handlers, it is essential for them to correctly interpret the breed standards, which are in effect descriptions of perfect dogs. We all know the perfect dog does not exist, but breed standards enable breeders and judges to select specimens as close to this ideal animal as possible.

A respected Australian dog judge once described a breed standard as "being at best a loosely worded document suitable only for the guidance of wise men and the instruction of fools". To ensure that one fits into the first of these two groups, I believe one should look back to when these blueprints for the breeds were first drawn up. If it is possible to ascertain why they were constructed, that makes simpler the task of appreciating both what they contain and how their authors intended them to be used. Setters had been developed and bred over hundreds of years without the need for a breed standard. Why then did enthusiasts of each breed feel compelled to commit to paper their breed's salient features? By looking at the dates when the first breed standards were drawn up, we may discover the reason. Traditionally, the setter had been bred for the purpose of working in the field. His sporting owners, many of whom maintained accurate stud books recording their dogs' genealogies over generations, had for years used selective breeding to improve their lines. Sportsmen who required their dogs to have substance and stamina naturally based breeding not on appearance, but on the hunting ability of the animals. This is not to say that atheistic qualities were never considered. In the case of Irish Setters, selective breeding with regard to colour was no doubt responsible for changing the breed from a predominantly white with red coloration to a red with white animal.

At the New Corn Exchange in Newcastle upon Tyne in England, on the 28th and 29th June 1859, a class for sporting dogs was added to the poultry show. Twenty-three Pointers and thirty-seven Setters competed for the prize of a brace of shotguns valued at twenty-five guineas[1]. The dog show had arrived, and with it breeding mainly for appearance would gradually come into favour. Unlike the situation in the field where animals were compared on their working ability, in the show ring the comparison was based purely on physical attributes. Due to an apparent lack of uniformity in appearance amongst setters exhibited, it was not uncommon for prizes at early shows to be withheld due to lack of merit. At the first Birmingham Exhibition of Sporting and Other Dogs in December 1860, the setters were divided into two classes, Irish Setters and other Setters. At the same event a year later, the setter classes were for the first time properly divided. There were classes for English Setters, Black and Tan Setters (as Gordons were then called), and Irish Setters (any size). Evidence of the lack of clear definition of true breed type is found in the fact that first and second place in the English Setter bitch classes went to two Gordon bitches. The explanation for this is that at that time there was an objection to a Black and Tan carrying any white, and those that did were automatically transferred to the English classes. Clearly there was a need to define what constituted true type for each breed.

There exists another more important catalyst for the adoption of breed standards apart from the desire to ensure uniformity in show ring assessment. All four setter breeds originated in a comparatively small area of the world and those enthusiasts associated with each breed's development (or in the case of the Red & White, re-establishment) would have been well known to each other. The industrial revolution in both the United Kingdom and America saw the rise of a new moneyed class eager to adopt the trappings and pursuits long held by the landed gentry, who were traditional owners of the breeds. Breeders were now being asked to export their stock. The new owners in far off places such as America and Australia were not privy to the background knowledge of the breed. They purchased the animal they saw in front of them without knowing what had been done over the years to achieve this end result. Breeders realised these new owners would have to have a set of guidelines to follow to ensure that the breed continued true to type in its new home. Standards that lay down the desirable qualities of both temperament and physical conformation inherent in character the breed would never be lost.

1945. Remor Irish Setters.

History of the Standard:

English Setters

The first book written specifically on setters is Edward Laverack's[2] *The Setter* which was published in 1872. Whilst it certainly did not establish an official breed standard, I am sure you will agree Laverack's views on the 'formation' of the English Setter constitute a blueprint for the breed: "Head long and light, not snake-headed, or deep flewed, but sufficiency of lip; remarkable for being very strong in the fore-quarters; chest deep, wide, and ribs sprung well behind the shoulders, carrying the breadth of back to where the tail is set on; immensely strong across the loins; shoulders very slanting or oblique; particularly short from the shoulders to where the hindquarters meet (I put it all in plain language, using no technical terms that perhaps some would not understand). A setter should not rise or be too upright in the shoulder, but level and broad; tail well set on in a line with the back, rather drooping, scimitar-shaped, and with plenty of flag; legs remarkably short, and

Ch. Peg O'My Heart, English Setter, owned by Silvermine Kennels. Photo by Joli. Courtesy of the Silvermine Collection.

very short from hock to foot and from knee to foot; feet close and compact; thighs particularly well bent or crooked, well placed and close under the body of the animal, not wide or straggling. Colour black, or blue and white ticked; coat long, soft and silky in texture; eyes soft, mild and intelligent, of a dark hazel colour; ears low set on and close to the head, giving a round development to the skull." On 1st December 1890 the English Setter Club was founded, with its objective, as recorded in the minutes of the first meeting, 'the improvement of the English Setter not only in regard to perfection of form, etc., but in respect to practical use in the field.'[3]

Irish Setters

In 1885 a group of Irish Setter enthusiasts formed the Irish Red Setter Club, Dublin, which on March 29th 1886 drew up the first authoritative breed description, complete with a scale of points for judging, which read as follows:

Head	10 points
Eyes	6 points
Ears	4 points
Neck	4 points
Body	20 points
Hind legs & feet	10 points
Fore legs & feet	10 points
Tail	4 points
Coat & feather	10 points
Colour	8 points
Size, style & General App.	14 points

The Irish Setter Association was formed in London in 1908 and adopted the breed standard of the Dublin Club. In 1930 the standard was revised in Dublin, establishing a slightly revised point scale and adding the category of 'Style', which read thus: "Must be racy, full of quality and kindly in expression." During the 1930's, when the English Kennel Club took responsibility for all the breed standards in the United Kingdom, the scale of points was dropped. The Kennel Club

Australian Ch. Quailmoor Georgia Brown, Irish Setter.
Owned by Norma Hamilton.

adopted a revised standard in 1986. This new standard did not change any of the important points of the existing standard, but simply clarified some details. The Irish Setter Club of America was formed in 1891, three years before the American Kennel Club was founded. One of the first actions of this new breed club was to adopt the "Standard and points of judging the Red Irish Setter" written by the Dublin club in 1886. Slight modifications were made to the original in 1895, 1908 and 1919.The revision adopted in 1960 no longer contained the scale of points. The latest version was adopted in 1990[4].

Irish Red and White Setter

Although the Irish Kennel Club adopted the first official standard for the breed in the 1940's, the Red and White is certainly not a new setter. The parti-coloured setter has a long history. Indeed, it is the older of the two varieties of setters native to Ireland. At the Birmingham show in 1860, the first show with a separate section for Irish Setters, the majority of those shown were red and white. However by 1875, the year the great Elcho was shipped to America, of the 66 Irish Setters exhibited at the Dublin show, 43 were solid red in colour. By the end of the century the solid red had so eclipsed his red and white cousin that the latter was almost extinct. During the 1920's[5] attempts were made to revive the breed, with the first Club being formed in 1944. The current club, The Irish Red & White Setter Field & Show Society was founded in 1981.

Irish Red and White Setter Ch. Sheebhin Bairre, owned by Canon Patrick Doherty, 1990.

Gordon Setter

Gordon Setter Ch. Blakeen Saegryte, 1940. Owned by George Thompson.

The Gordon Setter Club was founded in 1891, and after a lull was reformed in 1927 as the British Gordon Setter Club, which adopted its first breed standard in 1929.

Credit must go to the breed clubs, the custodians of the breed standards, for the fact that there has been very little change in standards over the years. They are still very much as originally written. One thing, however, has changed greatly over the same period and needs to be considered by today's users: it is the use of language. The writers chose their words carefully and, as was the current language practice, words were meant literally. Today we use words loosely, and indeed some words have completely changed meaning. What if the writers had described the Gordon Setter as an awful dog? Would we interpret that using today's accepted usage of awful or would it have meant full of awe? If we are looking for the exact meaning of something defined in a breed standard, we must understand the word as it was intended at the time of writing. Also worth noting is that the original authors of the standards were often associated with horses as well as dogs. Most people of the times were well familiar with equine terminology, and this accounts for the use of such terms in the standards. Describing the Gordon as "a weight carrying hunter" referred not to an ability to carry heavy game, but to his appearance. For people long associated with fox hunting such a description was extremely clear, denoting an animal that displayed both strength and endurance as opposed to the lighter built thoroughbred who was bred for speed over a short distance. The Irish Setter is described as "racy", a term which today some find difficult to interpret. For some it translates as lightweight, lean, and—all too often—as thin as possible; yet the dictionary defines racy as' vigorous, lively and spirited', which, if one thinks in terms of horses, is the intended meaning[6].

The Irish Setter, Plunkett, whelped in 1868, a grandson of Hutchinson's Bob and bred by the Hon. D. Plunkett. Purchased by Purcell Llewellyn who later sold the dog in the United States. Described as being small, rather light in color, Plunkett's pace was very great and his style was superior to all others in the field. Famous as a field and bench dog in England and the United States. Courtesy of Mrs. Anne Bolus.

Examination of what features a specimen of a breed should not display can also tell us something of the historical background of that breed. Aware that by exporting their animals they were passing custodianship of the breed to a new generation of breeders, the writers of the standards were equally careful to list traits that should be avoided. Today we take for granted those points found in all four setter breed standards that specify unwanted characteristics, but why did the writers feel compelled to include them in the first place? The common ancestry of all four setter breeds was far more recent than the spaniels which figured in their early development. Sportsmen striving to breed the perfect hunting dog often thought nothing of interbreeding the setter breeds including the now extinct black Welsh Setter. For example, one of the first importations to America was a dog called Plunkett, an Irish Setter. The common practise of crossing the setter breeds is exemplified by recorded matings of Plunkett with Carrie (English) and Nell (Gordon). Edward Laverack regarded by many as the founder of the modern English Setter was known to have introduced outside blood to improve the field work of his dogs. Laverack borrowed from the Irish Setter a fairly substantial amount of blood, and to a lesser degree borrowed from the Gordon.

Indeed, crossbreeding with animals outside the setter family was not unknown. W.N. Hutchinson[7] refers to a widely known instance of such crossbreeding by the Duke of Gordon. The Duke appears to have been so impressed by the hunting ability of a Collie bitch owned by one of his shepherds that in the 1870's he used her to improve the hunting prowess of his line of Black and Tans. The resulting litter produced six pups, all black tan and white. That the writers of the Gordon standard specifically listed "Collie type" as a fault is indicative of the need they saw to avoid animals that threw back to such cross breeding. The same need and reason is no doubt behind the naming of "Bloodhound type" as undesirable.

By specifying characteristics that were to be discouraged or even disqualifying, the standards writers were endeavoring to ensure that the four setter breeds remained distinct. Nowhere is this more evident than in the matter of colour for each of the breeds. The Irish was to display "no trace of black". It was not uncommon for dogs classified as Irish Setters to be the off-spring of crossing with Gordons. A successful show dog of the 1860's was Carlo, a red setter with black ear tips indicative of a Gordon Cross. Knowing that the red Irish Setter had only recently been separated from his red and white cousins, one clearly understands why the amount of permissible white was so minimal. Unless breeders remained vigilant in regard to this, the solid red dog could easily return to his parti-colored background.

The discouragement of body patches on English Setters could stem from a number of factors. Some would have it that this was intended to control the influence of his Spaniel ances-tors, but I believe there were more recent reasons for such discouragement. Today, for example, one immediately thinks of the Irish Setter as a solid red dog, yet it was not always the case; indeed they were not as is commonly thought only red and white. In 1845 a sporting writer, Youatt, recorded the colour of Irish Setters as being " either very red or red and white or lemon coloured, or white patched with deep chest-nut." Indeed two of the early Irish recorded in the *National American Kennel Club Stud Book* (1878) are Tom (650) who was lemon, and Speed (650), a black and white animal. For another thing, the English's ticked or 'Belton' markings were unique, and by discouraging body patches the standards writers were ensuring the continuance of this distinctive feature.

Although the standard of the Red and White is compara-tively recent (1940's) it displays the same logic behind its choice of characteristics to discourage or, in the case of colour, to disqualify. This breed was partly revived starting in the 1920's by the use of red Irish Setter field-type dogs that carried white markings. Once such assistance had been received it was necessary to breed away from any characteristics of this borrowed blood. Hence we find the head specifically is defined as not "showing the occipital protuberance, as in the Irish Red

Setter." The animal must be predominantly white to ensure that the breed remains distinct. Likewise any roaning or flecking on other than specified areas is cause for disqualification.

Standards Around the World

Breed standards[8] in use throughout the world are generally those adopted by one of three controlling bodies, American, English (Britain, Australia, New Zealand) or Federation Cynologique Internationale (Europe, Ireland, South America). When reading these three bodies, standards for all the breeds, one is struck by the fact that they are still very much the same, although those approved by the American Kennel Club contain much more detailed descriptions than either the British or F.C.I. standards. Australia, whilst adhering to the English standards, has adopted the concept of extended breed standards to flesh out the description. It must be pointed out, however, that there is one important area of difference in the Irish Setter standards, and that is height. Like the original drawn up for the breed, the English standard still has no reference to size or other dimensions. The American standard includes a guide to height and weight, calling for 27 inches and 70 pounds for dogs and 25 inches and 60 pounds for bitches. The F.C.I. is very different in that it has recently included an addendum to standardise heights to 23.5 to 26.5 inches for males and 21.5 to 24.5 inches for bitches. This standardisation is to take place over a 12-year period during which animals outside the prescribed height ranges are not to be penalised.

Breed standards are living documents, not historical writings of little relevance. Today, of course, setters are bred more for house pets and showing than for use in the field, but that must in no way be allowed to alter the standard. Whether the setter is used as a working gundog, an obedience trial competitor, a show dog, or a faithful companion and family member, he is not a true specimen of his breed unless he conforms to the breed standard. Whether breeders or judges have the greater responsibility to ensure this is a question often argued. Judges can judge only those animals entered in their classes, so some would argue that the main responsibility lies with the breeders. Yet in picking a winner judges often make that animal 'popular' for breeding. The standard is merely a word map or blueprint of the breed; it establishes relatively clear guidelines, but still leaves room for personal interpretation. Yet these standards must remain 'the bible' for judges and breeders alike. The former must always ensure that they select the animal that most closely adheres to the ideal laid out therein, whilst the latter group must ensure that they select breeding stock on the basis of the standard and not the current big winner in the show ring. If both groups do this consistently, the setter breeds will remain true to the type defined by the breed developers and custodians who have gone before.

Endnotes

1   Hutchinson, W., (editor), *Dog Encyclopedia*, 1935, Hutchinson, London

2   *The Setter: With Notices of the Most Eminent Breeds Now Extant; Instructions How to Breed, Rear and Break; Dog Shows, Field Trials, General Management, etc.*

3   Hubbard, C.L.B., *The English Setter Handbook*, 1958, Nicholson & Watson, London

4   Gardner, E., *Irish Setters Today*, 1998, Ringpress, Lydney UK

5   Hutchinson, W., (editor), *Dog Encyclopedia*, 1935, Hutchinson, London

6   Hutchinson, W., (editor), *Dog Encyclopedia*, 1935, Hutchinson, London

7   Hutchinson, Lieut.-Gen. W. N., *Dog Breaking*, 1869, John Murray, London

8   Refer to Appendix for current standards

1930. Stainton Kennels Showvan English Setters and Pointers. England.

8 | Presenting Setters In the Show Ring

*M*ost people learn to handle a dog by watching others at dog shows, by going to handling classes, and by finding out from experience what to do in the ring. Also, several excellent books and guides offer instruction in how to handle a dog. These are important sources for any beginner and they may also provide the experienced exhibitor with a helpful refresher course. However, they are usually general guidelines relevant to all breeds presented at dog shows. **This chapter will present a different approach to handling and will focus on the unique knowledge and skills a person must have to handle setters in the ring today.**

First, it is necessary to discuss what the role of the handler is. At AKC shows a judge has about two and one half minutes to examine each dog in the ring. In order to achieve that goal, the judge relies on handlers (both professional and amateur) to present the dog in a manner that facilitates the process of judging. That means that a handler needs to be familiar with the rules of the ring, how to pose the dog for examination, and how to move the dog in the different patterns that are requested by the judge. Preparation, training and practice with the dog are, of course, important if the handler is to comply in a timely manner with the judge's requests.

Next, a skillful handler must also be an advocate for the dog she or he is handling. There are two basic ways to achieve this:

- Handle the dog as is correct and appropriate for the breed.
- Handle the dog by accentuating its strong points and minimizing its weak points.

But in order to know how to accomplish either of these the handler of each breed—in this case the handler of each breed of setter—must know and apply the standard. In other words **the standard is not only the criterion used for judging; it is also a fundamental approach to skillful handling**. For example, each breed standard begins with an overview of what the breed was used for, what the dog should look like, and how the dog should act. The handler will learn that all the setters were bred to be hunters and they were reliable in responding to commands, but they also needed to show initiative in the pursuit of birds. Therefore, setters must be presented in the ring as responsive dogs that are able to stand proudly with little guidance from the handler. In motion, setters must be shown in a manner to allow them to look the part of an outgoing, intelligent, energetic dog. A skillful handler can achieve that "look" by posing the setter and fading into the background so that the dog appears all-important, and then moving the dog on a loose lead and so permitting the dog to appear capable on its own. Of course this takes practice, but it does have its rewards.

The handler must then read the fine points of the standards to learn what pose is appropriate for the breed. Although all the setter breed standards call for the tail to be level as an extension of the back, the Irish Setter standard describes a dog with a sloping top line. These descriptions become guidelines for the handler. The tail is to be held level for all the breeds and the top lines of the English, Gordon and Irish Red and White are to be level or very slightly sloping. Common to all four breeds is the general conformation that includes the front legs well under the body and the hocks perpendicular to the ground. To achieve this in the show ring, a wise handler will practice at home in front of a mirror installed at floor level or enlist a family member to be a "coach" until the right position for the dog is determined. Further, a handler can hold the head in a level position (the parallel lines of the skull and the muzzle are also parallel to the ground) to achieve the maximum arch to the neck and the maximum angle to the shoulder. The most difficult task a handler has when studying the standard is how to apply the words to a setter in motion. All the breeds call for the dog to carry its head high but the reason for this description must be understood. It presupposes a dog which takes its scent not from the ground, but from the air. However, when the dog is in the show ring traveling at a trot, holding the head high on a tight lead hampers the dog's ability to reach forward with a long stride. The skilled handler should give the dog some freedom to use its head in order to move in the efficient manner described in the standard.

The next use of the breed standard is to guide the handler in making the most of the individual dog he or she is handling. Since all dogs are different, it is impossible to show the dog to its best advantage if the handler follows the same routine with each dog. Therefore, the student of the standard will determine what are the best features of this dog. For example, when the dog's strong point is a lovely head and a good front, the handler must present the head with no distractions, and leave plenty of space so the judge has a full and clear view of the front. However, when the dog has a fault such as a soft back, emphasizing the correct angle of the neck, the level position of the head, and supporting position of the legs can limit the degree to which the weakness will be noticeable.

Again, it is the dog in motion that is the most difficult for a handler to evaluate. Finding the best speed in motion for the individual dog is essential for presenting the dog at its best. Dogs with less angulation will be limited in the reach and extension of the legs and therefore a moderate speed will be more effective. In each of the four setter breeds are individual dogs that pace or side-wind, problems that are caused by faults in the structure of the dog. Fortunately, trial and error practice sessions using different speeds and different methods of turning in front of the judge can limit or correct these gaiting problems. But first the handler must know what is happening, and that means the help of a friend, preferably a friend with a video camera. A good handler is a careful student of the breed standards.

During the 1930's, 40's and 50's a style of handling setters was formalized by skilled amateur and professional handlers. The style was based on a knowledge and application of the standard, but it also included the presentation of the setter as singularly elegant with the handler as a poised yet unobtrusive technician. The handler was to make every motion look smooth and easy. Every move of the handler had a reason, and the fewer the handler's moves, the greater the emphasis on the dog. There were professional handlers with setters who became legend for their skill and their "hands" on a dog. Benny Lewis, Harry Hill, Harold Correll, and perhaps the best of them all, Charlie Palmer. But there also emerged an even more elegant style of handling setters, and that was brought to the fore by Virginia Tuck and later by Paula McAteer. These two women owned the dogs they handled, and while they continued the classic style of handling setters, they added a grace and beauty to the ring that had not been seen in the male dominated sport.

Virginia Tuck and her husband Davis Tuck owned Silvermine Kennels where they bred English Setters. Her handling style had a profound affect on a whole generation of amateur and professional setter handlers, most of whom are now judges. Her ethics in the sport and her deportment at shows and other dog related functions, set a model to be copied. Anne Clark (Mrs. James E. Clark) said of Virginia Tuck, "She was the lady all women wanted to be like. She was the ultimate sportswoman and she was my role model in many ways—including

Virginia Tuck Hall. Courtesy of the Silvermine Collection.

how to handle a dog, but most importantly how to be a person of good character and gracious manners during a public life in competition." Jane Forsyth also recalled how Virginia Tuck set the bar higher for all setter owners and handlers. "She was so good at what she did for a dog both in and out of the ring that in order to win we all had to look better, act better and be more proficient as handlers."

A more civil, respectful climate in the show ring replaced the overt maneuvering for position and attention that had been the forte of many of the old time handlers. Art Baines, the famous Gordon handler, explained that when the old boys tried to push Ginny out of the line up she just smiled her most gorgeous smile, stood her ground, handled her dog to perfection and usually ended up the winner. Men and women both were influenced by her ability and her presence in the ring and she made it easier for the next generation of newcomers to enter the sport of dogs with confidence. The handling lessons that follow in this chapter are based on what Virginia Tuck demonstrated and what she advised others to do when handling setters in the show ring. Her style became the classic style.

But in a recent interview with Virginia Tuck (now Mrs. Leighton Hall), she said that it was not very easy to learn how to handle a dog. She said that it took her four years of hard work, practice, observation, and asking questions before she got that first ribbon. She learned to groom a dog by watching Harry Hill and Phil Marsh—handlers who believed in using their hands first and using grooming tools when necessary. It takes a lot of time to trim a dog so that it looks wonderful in a natural way. And then she talked of the finest English she ever had, Ch.Rhett Butler of Silvermine, and the most difficult dog she ever handled, the top winning Ch. Silvermine Wagabond. To observers at ringside Wagabond never put a foot wrong, and he moved, according to Elsworth Howell with "inspiration." Now we know that his owner and handler provided the inspiration.

While the English Setter ring had its star, the Irish Setter ring began to notice an up-and-coming talent in Paula McAteer. She had it all: she was tall, beautiful, graceful, elegantly dressed, and she had quiet skillful hands on a dog. She must have

Paula McAteer with Ch. Red Star of Hollywood Hills.
Courtesy of the McAteer Collection.

known that she was the attention-getter in the ring, but she handled her dog in such a manner that she herself became background. She also came into the sport of dogs as a novice when she became engaged to John. "The date of our wedding in 1940 was changed from September to October so he could show his Ch. Wamsutta Onondaga at Westchester. After the war when John was released from the Army at Fort Ord, California, I bought a puppy for him to celebrate his return. Ward Gardner was at Mrs. Cuthbertson's the day I picked out the dog I was to handle from puppy classes to Best In Show, Int. Ch. Red Star of Hollywood Hills, CDX—and that was just the beginning." (other comments on Irish Setters by Mrs. McAteer appear elsewhere in this book).

Many other handlers both amateur and professional have contributed to the success of setters over the years and photos of some are included here. But Joyce and Athos Nilsen became the most successful of all setter handlers in the breeding, raising, and handling of English, Gordon and Irish Setters. Thenderin became a force all to itself as the largest Irish Setter Kennel in the United States, and they stamped a type on a line of dogs that endures to this day. Their handling prowess was legend, their success is unmatched.

Joyce Nilsen with Ch. Thenderin William Muldoon.
Courtesy of Thenderin Kennels.

Ann Rogers Clark and Jane Kamp Forsyth, Boston, 1957.
Judge: Mrs. Geraldine Rockefeller Dodge.

Photo by Schaffer.
Courtesy of the Silvermine Collection.

Neil Weinstein with Ch. Guys' N Dolls Shalimar Duke.

*Ross Petruzzo with
Ch. MacNeal of
Ellicott. Judge: John
Lawreck. Photo by
Gilbert. 1974.*

*Charles Oldham with Ch. Linlees
Glen Garrie. Photo by Ludwig.*

*Arthur and Audrey Baines with Afternod Gordon Setters.
Courtesy of Wilcox.*

C. Bede Maxwell (Maxie) with Ch.
Enzed Laurent at the Melbourne Royal,
Australia, 1955.

Tom Tobin with Ch. Webline Fame
and Fortune. 1972.

William Trainor with
Canadian & American Ch.
Arundel's Duke of Norfolk.
New York, 1973.
Photo by Klein.

Joyce began handling setters as a very young woman in the East before coming to California. Tall and attractive, she used her knowledge of how a dog is built to establish a method of handling that enhanced her great dogs and confounded the judges of her lesser charges. As a handler, Joyce Nilsen could provide a setter that was lacking with the appearance of balance. She was a technician who always knew both where the foot should be placed and how it made a difference to the look of the whole dog. Her success, according to George Brodie, came from "an infinite knowledge of the breed and an intense desire to improve what she had and how she presented it."

How To Handle A Setter

The following set of illustrations and instructions are offered to help the novice handler, the Junior Showmanship handler, and the Junior Showmanship judge understand the breed-specific method of handling setters in the show ring. The setter presentation style is based on tradition established by the great amateur and professional setter handlers of the early and mid twentieth century. These handlers believed that the words and meaning of the breed standards determined how the dog should be shown. They also believed that they were responsible for presenting each dog in its best possible form both in pose and in motion. Distractions created by the handler that take the judges focus away from the dog or that do not facilitate the judge's examination of the dog have always been perceived as a fault. The use of various presentation styles that put the dog in a position that does not enhance it's form and is not appropriate to how the setter should look limits the dog's best appearance. Further, the appearance of the handler which includes confidence, poise, posture, coordinated motion with the dog and professional attire for the sport, is important. The great amateur and professional handlers of today know the standard and know how to evaluate the dog they are handling. They spend time training and practicing until the correct position, speed of motion and coordinated plan of action has been worked out in detail so that the setter can appear in the ring commanding the attention it deserves.

Moving the Dog in a Circle

Take the lead in your left hand and gather the surplus inside your hand. Make one loop over your forefinger and put your thumb on top so that the lead can not slip.

With your right hand, hold the dog's head in a level position and bring the collar of the lead around and under the dog's ear. While the type of lead is a personal decision, selection should be based on the size, strength and comfort of the dog. For example, the use of a choke collar may be unwise on some dogs because they react by traveling with the head to one side to escape the discomfort.

With the lead in place signal to your dog that you are ready to begin—a pat on the chest is one way to do this.

Begin with three long, walking strides to help the dog begin moving smoothly.

Accelerate your pace to a run. Look forward to check for distance and direction and look back over your shoulder to make sure the dog is running straight.

Moving the Dog Individually

With long confident strides and the lead placed in the correct position on the dog's neck take the dog out beyond the judge and turn the dog around in front of the judge until the dog is facing in the opposite direction and is ready to move in a straight line. This should be done so that the dog is in constant motion.

Move the dog directly away from the judge. The handler of an adult setter should take a large step coming out of the turn so that the dog is not held back from advancing speed.

After three long strides accelerate your speed to a run while keeping plenty of space between you and the dog.

The speed of motion should be determined by the correct speed for the dog. Practice at home and the use of a video tape will help the handler determine the best speed for the individual dog.

When moving your dog in an L or triangle-pattern, guide the dog so that it is moving in straight lines. Stationary reference points help handlers determine straight lines.

When returning to the judge at full speed give the dog space and begin to tighten the lead for control.

Change from a run to walking steps to slow the dog down before the stop. Bring the dog in closer and on a shorter lead for maximum control, and stop in front of the judge keeping the dog in a head-on position. Leave enough room so that you can walk the dog into the best position for the front legs and feet.

An alternative method of stopping the dog in front of the judge is to allow the dog to stand in a natural position. Use bait ONLY if it does not distort the face, muzzle, flews and ear set of the dog. While the head and expression of the setter is very important, so too is the unencumbered view of the dog by the judge. Use bait ONLY if you keep it out of sight and your hands and arms out of the way. Do not hold bait between the dogs mouth and the judges hands. If you must use bait keep your hand low so that the dog's head is level and the neck is arched forward.

Stop the dog for a posed position. Slip your right hand underneath the dog's muzzle keeping the head level, put the thumb and forefinger inside the neck piece of the lead.

With one motion bring the lead forward and clear of the dog. Put the lead next to your own right foot. Place the dog in a posed position.

Posing the Dog for Examination

As the judge approaches, present the head for examination. Leave space between you and the dog.

Upon the judge's request, show the bite so that the front teeth and the side teeth are in clear view.

Some judges prefer to see the bite in an open flexed position so that the front lower teeth can be evaluated.

The most efficient way to pose a dog is to have the dog walk into its own weight distribution. Position the head with the muzzle parallel to the ground and adjust the front feet if necessary—place judge's side front leg first followed by handler's side front leg next.

Grasp the front leg at the elbow making sure to place the foot back under the dog.

After the front legs are placed and while keeping the head in a level position and the neck arched forward, place the judge's side rear leg first.

Place the handler's side rear leg and then check the position of all legs, check the topline, and level of head and angle of the neck.

With the dog in the correct position for the breed and the optimum position for the individual dog, kneel with one knee down and leave plenty of space between you and the dog. Tip the dog's head slightly toward the judge and hold the tail level or slightly lower than the topline. These details are important.

You should appear balanced, relaxed and comfortable in every phase of presenting the dog. Keep one foot on the ground so you are able to rise easily. Keep your back straight and your head high so that you can see all parts of the dog and what is happening in the ring.

The final presentation of the dog is based on prior study of the dog's strong points and weak points. It is also based on the style of pose appropriate to the individual breed. For example, in this illustration the Irish Setter should be placed in a position so that the topline is more sloping. An English Setter and Gordon Setter has a level top line and a Red and White should have a level topline in examination but the heavy coat around the withers, neck and fore-chest makes it appear slightly sloping.

Demonstration of Handling by Christopher Radcliffe. Photos by R.S. Brown.

Setters and their Owners in Junior Showmanship

The following is a definition and purpose as published by The American Kennel Club in *Junior Showmanship Regulations Judging Guidelines and Guidelines for Juniors*:

> Junior Showmanship classes are non-regular classes which are judged solely on the ability and skill of Juniors in handling their dogs as in the breed ring. The purpose of Junior Showmanship Competition is twofold: to introduce and encourage Juniors to participate in the sport of dogs; and to provide Juniors with a meaningful competition in which they can learn, practice, and improve in all areas of handling skill and sportsmanship.[1]

The American Kennel Club also offers guidelines for Juniors competing:

> Juniors are important to the sport of dogs. Juniors who learn about good sportsmanship, dogs, handling and dog shows will be valuable to the sport in the future. Junior Showmanship classes

are offered at most dog shows. These classes are held so that young people can: experience winning and losing among those who are similar in age, learn the correct way to handle the breed they own, practice handling skills in competition, improve the way they handle their own dog, and prepare for handling the dog in regular classes.

Junior Showmanship classes are judged on the ability of the Junior to handle his or her dog. The quality of the dog is not judged. Juniors will be asked to demonstrate the following: moving the dog with the rest of the class, presenting the dog in the standing position proper to its breed, and moving the dog individually in a regular pattern.

Juniors are expected to know basic ring routines. They should be able to follow directions, use space wisely, and be familiar with gaiting patterns. Juniors should appear "ring wise," alert to what is going on in the ring, and should be prepared for changes in the routine of judging.

JUNIORS MUST BE ABLE TO CONTROL THEIR DOGS AT ALL TIMES. Any Junior who cannot control his or her dog will be excused by the judge.

The appearance of Juniors should be clean, neat, and well-groomed. They should wear clothing that is comfortable to handle in and appropriate for dog shows. Clothing should not distract, limit or hinder the judge's view of the dog.

Dogs should be groomed and trimmed as they would be for the breed ring. Judges will not evaluate the quality of the grooming and trimming, but Juniors should make an effort to prepare their dogs for the ring. Unnecessary grooming of the dog in the ring to gain attention is not proper conduct.

Juniors should appear confident, prepared, business-like and attentive. They should be courteous to both the judge and other Juniors. Juniors are expected to handle their dogs without disturbing the dogs of the other Juniors. Juniors should not crowd and they should not disturb others by continued use of toys and bait. Juniors should be alert to the needs of their dogs. They should use firm but thoughtful hands in controlling and handling their dogs. Juniors should not be impatient or heavy-handed.

Juniors will be judged on their ability to present their dogs in the same way the dog is properly handled in the breed ring. Juniors will also be judged on their ability to make their individual dog look its best in both pose and motion. During all parts of the competition Juniors should handle their dogs in a quiet, smooth, efficient manner. Juniors should strive to make the DOG stand out as the most important part of the team effort.

Junior handlers should be able to keep the dog's attention without using dramatic or unnecessary movements, gait the dog in a controlled trot without distracting or interfering with the judge's view of the dog, be aware of what is going on in the ring, and concentrate on the dog and not the judge.

Junior handlers who use exaggerated posture, motions or gestures in any part of the competition will be faulted.[2]

Since Children's Handling began in 1932 and Junior Showmanship was recognized in 1971 by the AKC as an official class at dog shows, Juniors and their setters have been at the forefront of the sport and in the spotlight at the winners circle.

Handling a setter correctly for the breed gives a Junior an advantage in being able to present the dog in a manner that has been established and respected for at least seventy five years. Further, the setter is an attention-getter and enhances the Junior's chances to be noticed. However, the handling of the setter is not easy. It does not rely on bait or the use of a lead for a posed position and it requires the Junior to manage a dog that may appear to be bigger and stronger than the Junior. But Juniors and setters are a natural partnership and when they enter the finals ring at Westminster they will be noticed.

Some of the Juniors over the years who established excellence in handling in Junior Showmanship are Westminster winners Walter Wilson, Gordon Setter 1943; Bethny Hall Mason, Irish Setter 1959; Betty Lou Ham, Irish Setter 1961; and Randy McAteer, Irish Setter 1977.

Beginning young.
Photo by Kohler.
1993.

Juniors must be accurate in their presentation of a setter. Photo by Callea.

Ray Sumida, Best Junior Showman in California. 1956. Photo by January.

Kristin Karboski, Westminster Finalist, 1998.

*Peter Kubacz, Westminster
Finalist, 1998. Photo by
Ashby.*

*Donovan Plummer handling his Irish Red and White
Setter, Chester, to a top win at National Specialty,
2000. He is also the top winning Junior for Red &
Whites.*

Kristin Karboski handling her Gordon Setter under Roy Holloway. Photo by Tatham, 1997.

Randy McAteer, Westminster Winner 1977, with Judge, James Edward Clark.

Emily Bisso winning Best in Junior Showmanship. 2000. Photo by Cott.

Taffe Walker McFadden and her Fantail's Mandarin Orange. Chilliwack, B.C., Canada, 1977. Photo by Hodges.

Anne Green with her English Setter at Westminster.

Endnotes

1   American Kennel Club's Junior Showmanship Judging Guidelines (Section 1)

2   American Kennel Club's Guide to Junior Showmanship Competition for Juniors (Sections 1-6)

1968 Junior Handler Lesley Rosen with her BOS Ch. Canberra Blue Shadow. Judge William R. Trotter.

9 | Judging the Setters

*T*he art of good dog show judging is the quick, correct evaluation of the merits of pure-bred dogs." [1] Correct judging requires knowledge of the anatomical parts of the dog as it stands and in motion. It also requires the knowledge of the specific characteristics of the individual breed being assessed.

All four setter breeds are judged by standards that are written to preserve the hunting ability of the dog as it was developed for work on a particular terrain. Over the years observers have come to see these practical or work related characteristics as beautiful. One reason why these breeds have endured is that the aesthetic points of the setter are not "fancy points" as in other breeds, but rather represent essential components integral with the function of the dog. A second reason may be that people see beauty in nature, and these very old breeds are part of natural and cultural awareness.

Further, the judging of setters—as with all dogs—is a comparative, cognitive exercise that employs subjective decision making, and as such involves both intellectual and emotional factors. The judge must therefore possess detailed knowledge of established criteria, canine structure, and the obvious and subtle differences in each of the setter breeds, and must studiously avoid any subjectivity that reflects whim, fancy, or the mood of the day. Therefore, good judges must have knowledge based on experience and be willing to take on the challenge of accepting from the literature, the sport, and from colleagues new knowledge that adds to an ever-increasing proficiency. Hand in hand with the increased skill must be developed of useful and sound criteria that move subjectivity

toward legitimacy and consistency. The purpose of this chapter is to discuss what judges must know and how they can
learn it, and what experienced judges offer in the way of
informing the fancy about the breeds of setters today.

What Setter Judges Must Know

In a book that should be required reading for all judges,
Thelma and Curtis Brown perceptively stated, **"Dog judging
is like a game of hide and seek—the dog's owner has several
months in which to plan how to conceal undesirable points;
the judge in the ring has two minutes to find them."** [2] Dog
judging is not easy: it is not a task for equivocator nor for the
overly confident. It certainly is not for those who lack experience in dogs in general and setters in particular.

Fine judges come from many backgrounds, none of which
is superior. Some judges have had long and successful careers
as professional handlers, and are skilled in the arts of dog hus-
bandry, show preparation, and presentation. They bring to
judging a broad knowledge of pure-bred dogs and an insight
of what happens in the show ring. They also may bring with
them, however, a viewpoint overly affected by competition,
show records, positive and negative biases toward judges,
handlers, and breeders—and in some cases a superficial knowledge of setters because their experience is based on only a few
individual dogs. It takes time to transfer from one occupation
in the sport of dogs to another, but most handlers in time do
this very, very well.

Other judges come from the ranks of breeders and
exhibitors, some of whom have also been proficient amateur
handlers. These judges have experience in one or several breeds
and have spent many years establishing a successful line of
dogs. They have knowledge of the breeding, raising, and training of dogs. Often they are members of local, regional, and
national dog clubs, and as such have the opportunity to
continue in educational workshops and seminars. These new
judges bring with them in-depth knowledge of specific breeds.
They understand the breed purpose, origins, show trends, and

unique characteristics; in most cases they have a broad view of the status of the breed at a given point. However, they too bring to judging positive and negative biases learned and reinforced over the years, and they may find it difficult to make hard decisions among those who have been peers for many years. Also, they may be too specialized in their knowledge and experience. They may see the breed only in the context of the breed itself. In order fully to appreciate one breed, the effective judge must be able to see it in comparison and contrast to other breeds. The application of compare/contrast is particularly essential in the judging of setters.

In addition, there are among the most respected judges today individuals who have been both professional handler and breeder. In most cases they bring to the ring the best possible blend of knowledge and experience. Still, even these judges face the inevitable and often awkward transfer from one side of the ribbons to another. Therefore, the first thing new judges must learn is that they cannot know everything, nor are they expected to. Every judge learns from judging; and whether it is a match, a sweepstakes, or the national specialty, the learning process goes on and knowledge is cumulative.

Setter judges must know and be able to apply the standard—and that means the actual words of the standard as well as its further explanation and analysis, not what the judge would like it to be. But even when the judge applies the standard, the sorting of dogs in a class is not a scientific endeavor. While the standard must always be the primary set of criteria upon which decisions are made, a judge must establish personal guidelines which, although subjective, have sound principles to support them. Some judges call them the "bottom line" or "when all else fails" or "where the buck stops." These personal criteria are used in difficult decision-making situations—for example when two fine dogs in a class are different from each other but equally deserving, and it has to be one or the other. Another such example would be when a class consists of four poor dogs that differ in areas of soundness and degree of type. If after the standard has been applied the dilemma still exists, a judge may use his or her own standard or good reason for the decision. Some judges ask, "Which dog represents the best example of the breed's purpose?" Others question, "Which dog looks like it could do a day's work in the bird field?" or, "Which dog would I rather admit to owning?" Yet another might say, "With the dogs equal in quality, I'll choose the one in the best physical condition?" These may be applied to finalize a placement but only after the standard is applied in full measure.

Of course, decisions made on grounds of personal taste and opinion are the least likely to be sound. The further the judge strays from the cognitive process of applying the standard and sound reasons, and strays to making decisions from the heart, the less consistent the judging will be.

Setter judges are responsible for applying the standard, and when they do so they are applying the knowledge of *type*. This term, as central as it is to our base of understanding in the sport of dogs, is unfortunately one of the most often misused. Type is described by Hayes Blake Hoyt in her famous article, "Four Definitions" [3] in the following way:

> "Type is the standard—the description of a breed based entirely on the purpose that particular kind of dog has to fulfill." In other words, the dog that most closely resembles its standard both in disposition and appearance is the most typical. Type is not the appropriate term for "moving correctly." A dog may move with efficiency in a generic way but until "correctly" is applied to breed specific requirements of motion, there is not a presence of type. Another misuse of the word is, "type is elegance." Yet, until elegance is defined and is described as a set of components within the accepted breed standard it cannot be called type. Many people say "I prefer that type" or that was a "typey bitch" to denote separation within a breed by using personal preference rather than using one standard of measure for all dogs within the breed. Type, then is the presence

of a group of specific in-depth breed characteristics that describe the original functional imperatives of each breed. Judges must be able to identify type. It has often been said by excellent judges that their process of sorting begins with selecting the most typical dogs from the entry and then from those selecting the most sound. Even then, it must be recalled that sound must be the correct soundness for that breed.

How The Judge Can Learn

Today more than ever before, opportunities for learning about pure-bred dogs are available everywhere. There are seminars, workshops, weekend college, and training sessions. These have replaced the methods that back in the mists of time—the 1940's and the 1950's—relied on word of mouth at the benching stalls and under the handlers' tent. While that learning method was effective and is now a fond nostalgia trip for some, it could not supply the needs of the burgeoning number of judges in the present sport of dogs.

And even given the many formal offerings in dog education, other important judging strategies should be noted. A judge should be able to carry in the mind's eye an ideal silhouette of the breed to be evaluated. The silhouette must be the correct representative of the breed in all details of the outline. It should be the ideal based on the description in the standard and not the fond memory of a famous dog of long ago. Although that famous dog may help the judge to build the silhouette, the shape itself must be the ideal in every way. Another way that a judge, especially an aspiring or new judge, can learn is to seek out a wide variety of people who are knowledgeable about setters. Among these should be handlers, breeders, judges and retired or emeritus judges. These people should not be limited to those with whom you agree. Learning takes place when judges are challenged to analyze diverse viewpoints. A studying judge should ask questions with an open mind and listen to the answers with an equally open mind. Finally, judges should use a variety of study methods

English Setter Silhouette

Gordon Setter Silhouette

English Setter

*The English Setter is level in topline and is slightly longer than it is tall. The head is **moderate** in size with less depth of skull and muzzle than the Gordon Setter and more depth of skull and muzzle than the Irish Setter. The planes of the head are parallel. The head shown above is correct but also correct is more depth of flew when it is in proportion with the skull and the substance of the whole dog. Balance of the front assembly with the rear assembly is key to correct structure. English Setters should have a well developed forechest or prosternum. Bone size is moderate and feet are well arched. The tail should be an extension of the level topline and should be presented and carried at the level of the back and not above. (Exact wording of the standards is in the appendix).*

Gordon Setter

The Gordon Setter is slightly sloping in topline with a level, short back (the back is measured from behind the withers to the beginning of the loin) and is described in the United States as more square than the other setters when measured from the point of the shoulder to the rear of the back leg. Because of the furnishings of the Gordon it will appear slightly longer than it is tall. The Gordon is slightly taller than the English Setter but not as tall as the Irish Setter. The characteristic unique to the Gordon is its degree of substance in bone and body development—that is more than the other setters but must never look cumbersome or coarse. The head, in skull and muzzle, is deeper (longer from the top of the skull to the bottom of the jaw line and longer from the top of the muzzle to the bottom line of the muzzle. The top of the skull because of its greater width than the other setters, may appear in profile as very slightly rounded but the planes of the head are parallel. The Gordon has a well developed forechest or prosternum, must appear up on leg to the extent that the height is in proportion with the overall length, and must be in correct balance between the forequarters and the rearquarters. Gordons that are exaggerated in any part that sets them out of balance are not correct. The feet, well arched, are larger and rounder than the other setters. The tail is presented as an extension of the topline and is to be carried level with the topline. (Exact wording of the standards is in the appendix)

Irish Red and White Setter Silhouette

Irish Setter Silhouette

Irish Red and White Setter

The Irish Red and White Setter is level in topline or may appear slightly sloping because the ruff of coat covering the shoulders gives the **impression** *of more height at the withers than at the rear (protuberance at the top of the upper pelvis). The head is unique and should not be compared to the other setters. Although the skull and muzzle are equal in length, the size and width of the skull as compared to the narrower width of the muzzle may create an impression that the muzzle is shorter. The presence of the occiput should be identified by touch but there is not a definition to be seen. The flews neatly cover the under jaw creating a tapered muzzle that is squared off at the end. Because the neck is to be left in a natural growth of coat it may appear shorter. Although the Red and White is slightly shorter in height than the English Setter, it will appear smaller because it carries less bone. The Red and White also appears smaller because it* **correctly** *carries much less length of coat. The balance between the running gear of front and rear is essential. What cannot be seen in the silhouette is the well-sprung rib cage which is larger than the other setters when evaluated in proportion to the whole dog. Legs are strong, feet are small and firm, and the development of bone is durable but is less in mass than the other setters. The tail, which is to be naturally coated, may appear longer than it actually is. This silhouette is an overall picture but the dog must be carefully examined by hand to assess its structure. (Exact wording of the standards is in the appendix)*

Irish Setter

The Irish Setter is sloping in topline and is slightly longer than it is high. The head is long, lean, and clean in lines. The skull and muzzle are close to the same width and are equal in length. The planes of the head and muzzle must be parallel. The flews cover neatly the development of the lower jaw and end in a squared end of the muzzle. Development of the forechest or prosternum is essential. The angulation of the front is deep so that the forelegs are set well under the dog and the line of the shoulder blade is sloped well back. The balance of the rearquarters with the front requires that the rear be correctly constructed without exaggerated length of any part of the assembly. The Irish must look as a dog standing over plenty of ground: Legs are long, strong and lean, feet are rather small. Standing naturally, the Irish must have short hocks that are perpendicular to the ground. The tail is presented as an extension of the sloping topline and is held slightly lower than the set on of the tail. It should be carried level or very slightly elevated as allowed in the American standard. (Exact wording of the standards is in the appendix)

including books, articles, brochures, lectures and videotape. And for a breadth of knowledge in how setters differ in their work, a judge should attend hunt tests, field trials, and Obedience trials.

A number of provisional judges surveyed in the process of preparing this book indicated that certain aspects of judging setters raise problems. The most common concern was the patches on English Setters. One judge admitted that to be on the safe side she had omitted from consideration the dogs with patches—any patches. But some patches are acceptable; some may even be "badges of honor." A tear drop whether large or small at the outside corner of the eye recalls the individual look of Wagabond or Kip, and it is the fond hope of many that a spot at the base of the tail will be seen as a direct link to Sturdy Max. Eye patches and patches above the ear are common occurrences in English Setters, and while they may not be the goal of a breeder, the markings are well within the standard. Body patches, however, are to be faulted; this criterion separates the English from the ancient inheritance factors linked to spaniels and possibly to the Red and White. In fact the Red and White limits what is perceived to be a connection to the English Setter, and therefore calls for clearly defined red islands or patches on a pure white background without ticking above the elbow and without ticking on the body.

Another worry for new judges is how to evaluate the markings on Gordon Setters. Some have a vague recollection that there is a color disqualification in this breed and therefore they are wary about each tan marking in each tan place. These concerns are separate. The disqualification is for dogs that are "predominantly tan, red or buff and which do not have the typical pattern of markings of a Gordon Setter." In other words, while the Gordon should have tan markings in the places designated in the standard, it is not a disqualification if each tan point is not present. It is a disqualification if the dog is primarily tan, red, or buff.

Other concerns that new judges have brought up are the method of evaluating the dog in motion. Most judges have studied foot fall patterns and can apply their knowledge to the actual dogs. However, judges are confused by the fact that the structure of many setters today, especially the Irish does not allow for the described foot fall. For example, with the over angulated rear structure in combination with a sloping croup, the dog's rear foot will not fall in the place that the front foot left empty. Instead it will overreach and interfere with the front. New judges are not sure how to evaluate this, since it is quite common, and since pictures in magazines and breed booklets show it to be true. Judges should be assured that the footfall pattern for all setters is correct when the dog is built correctly and the dog should be judged relative to the degree of the fault.

Contributions of Experienced Breeders and Judges

Charles Herendeen, former all-breed handler and now a judge, brings to the ring a lifetime of setter knowledge and experience. Some of his comments are presented here:

> I judge on a combination of type, balance, and soundness. For example, it must look like a Gordon and must not cross over to another breed or type is destroyed. It must look like a dog that can do real work—a dog like Sangerfield Jed. In addition, if one part of the dog is off it will affect other parts. If the dog is too big then the bone structure will be out of proportion. And if the hock is too long the whole rear will be lacking in efficiency. Today, handlers tend to stretch the setters into unnatural poses that do not serve the dog to its best advantage. Handlers also have decided to create a new fad in changing the natural underline of the coat. I don't like it. **But of greatest importance and of greatest concern is that the setters have changed in recent years yet the standards of the setters have remained the same.** This should be a warning. When the breeders do not follow the standard that has preserved the essence of the breed, there is a very real problem.

Jeannette Brady Shields with her husband, John Ward Brady, was the owner of Frenchtown Kennels, the home of the famous litter of eleven champions as well as many other English Setter stars. She was both a breeder and a proficient handler, a judge of all sporting and the judge of the first National Specialty for her own breed. Here is her testimony:

> Each breed of setter must be typical of its own shape and form. **Dogs and bitches must meet the criteria of the breed but must look like representatives of their own sex.** When presenting a dog in the ring it must be done so that the dog is all-important and that nothing interferes with the view of the dog. The trimming that is done must achieve a natural appearance. Fads of trimming look particularly inappropriate on a gundog. Baiting is a bad habit and brings out the worst appearance in the setter. A setter's beauty is first and foremost in the face and head and the use of bait distorts that beauty. What is also common to all the setters is that they should have a level tail carriage. I am particularly critical of soft pasterns—they are wrong on any gundog. When I judge I like to see the dog move in all directions: front, rear and side motion. I place emphasis on what I see when the dog moves in profile at a moderate speed.

Virginia Tuck Hall with her husband Davis Tuck bred and raised English Setters and English Cockers at Silvermine Kennels. They were both setter judges and authors. (see chapter eight on handling the setter) Mrs. Hall offers the following:

> One regret I have is that when I went to visit Blue Bar my guide was so thorough in escorting me through the stables, horse barns, paddocks and grooming areas that there was no time left in the schedule for me to see the dogs! Davis believed in the study of pedigrees and he carried a

portfolio of pedigrees with him to every show. We studied pedigrees, but we also studied the individual dog to try to ascertain what were the best choices for breeding. Therefore, one piece of advice I would give to present day dog breeders is to look back before proceeding forward. As far as presenting a dog in the ring, I never carried bait because I wanted my dog to look its best, but I did carry a dog comb which I used when the judge was not looking. As a judge I always wanted to be able to examine the dog thoroughly and it required extra time with setters because of the coat. **My advice to judges would be to use your hands to find everything. And don't be afraid to fault the coat if it has been damaged by improper grooming**.

Anne Rogers Clark was one of the most famous of all-American professional handlers, and she handled many setters during her career. She is now a highly respected all-breed judge. She advises judges and breeders with these words:

Of the three setters I find the English to be in the best shape today. There are, in particular, a number of young bitches that if used wisely, represent a possibility for even greater quality in the future. I am particularly concerned about the present status of the Irish Setter. Too many lack correct balance, and the main problem is the exaggerated formation of the rear that distorts type but also prevents the dog from being sound. They cannot stand with the hocks perpendicular. The coats in Irish are of good quality and for the most part presented in a natural appearance. The Gordons have reached a level of some consistency and adhere to the standard better than before. **But the coats on Gordons and English are now so profuse that the natural lines of the**

dog are often hidden. Also the texture of the coat on English and Gordon appear to be changed perhaps as a result of the frequent washings and the use of a blow dryer. Concerning all the setter breeds—while there have been gay tails in all the setters for a long time today the proportion of dogs with gay tails should be seen as a problem that distorts the look of the setter as a whole.

Paula McAteer with her husband, John McAteer has been a breeder of Irish Setters since 1945. (see Chapter 8). Paula shares her thoughts as follows:

The contributions of large breeding programs by kennels such as Kinvarra, Redbarn, Thenderin, Tirvelda and Knightscroft provided a vital breeding base that was important to the breed for two reasons. First, these kennels gave newcomers the opportunity to begin with line-bred stock and provided the breed with a variety of available studs which was a luxury that few small kennels could have afforded. Second, they provided opportunities for students of the breed to learn from owners who had "painted their setters red using a genetic pallette." Smaller kennels have also helped shape the breed—an example of which is Kimberlin owned by Claire Andrews for fifty years. I have spent over a half a century devoted to the Irish Setter and I have positive hopes for the future. But among my concerns for the breed is that there are extremes in size, with too many Irish either too big or too small. A lack of bone and substance is also missing as are lack of level head planes. **While there are some fine specimens today, there are also many that are unsound in the rear and this must be addressed—and soon.** I wonder, where are the balanced dogs of type for us to use today? Where are the Irish like Kermit, Muldoon, Star Rocket, Kyrie and Star?

Jane Forsyth, was for many years one of America's leading professional handlers before she began a judging career. Her experience with many of the great setters of the past has created a demand for her judging at numerous national and regional specialties. This is how she views setters today:

> Compared to other breeds, the setters are in pretty good shape. English Setter bitches are of excellent quality, but I don't know where the good males are. The consistency in type long absent from the Gordon appears to be stable. But the top coats of Gordons have too often earned the label "mow and show." In other words, cut off the top coat and take them into the ring. While I'm on the topic of coats, there are too many handlers who have decided to sculpt the bottom line of the setter feathering and I am going to continue to tell them, 'You're not helping the dog by trimming that way.' It should look NATURAL. **Also, there are too many Irish Setters that lack balance and proper head planes**. And did I tell you that I dislike English Setters with short legs?

Other veteran judges who have contributed comments directed toward new judges say that although they dislike the artificial methods used in trimming setters today, they would judge the dog as it is because the grooming is not a genetic problem. Also a common question is "where do they exercise these English and Gordon in the winter with their coats trimmed down to stubble?"

New judges for Red & Whites and that includes all setter judges in the United States will need to read this standard carefully. The heads are different. Unlike the other sporting dogs that are Red & White, this one has a black or dark brown nose and the coat color is a sparkling white background with deep chestnut red, the darker the better. Yes the dog is to have whiskers and the trimming is minimum—no electric clippers. Because the dog is to be presented in a natural coat judges must use their hands on this breed to discover the merit or faults.

Practical Suggestions for Setter Judges

When you are having problems trying to evaluate the setters, have the dog stand on its own without positioning and without bait. You will get the truth of how the dog uses its legs and feet and how the body weight is distributed. Examine bites with a flexed jaw (slightly open) so that you can see the bottom dentition. Evaluate the dog in motion. When it is going directly away, check to see if its body is traveling in a straight line. There should not be any twisting or untoward motion. When the dog is moving in profile, keep your eye on the back line. It should be smooth and steady, free from any rise and fall. The dog that lifts its feet high, usually in the front, is to be faulted. The foot should not rise higher than the height of the wrist. One last comment is about body roll. Keeping in mind that puppies often go through growth stages during which the loose flesh around the body tends to roll back and forth when the dog is in motion, check the dog for such contributing problems as lack of tuck up under the loin or too long or too flat a loin.

This chapter has presented information for judges, and while it is directed primarily toward beginning judges, others can learn from these long experienced members of the dog fancy. Judging is a formidable task and a serious responsibility. Judges should create a positive climate for those in the ring and outside the ring. As senior members of the fancy, judges should reach out with empathy and understanding to the newcomer, and treat all those in the ring with equality and respect. It should go without saying that they must accord their colleagues the respect and consideration they expect in return.

Endnotes

1 *The Art and Science of Judging Dogs* by Curtis M. Brown and Thelma R. Brown (1976)

2 Ibid.

3 Visualizations of the Dog Standard, (1977).

Laura Delano presenting Best of Breed to one of Louis Iacobucci's first Celous' champions at Troy, New York, 1959. Photo by WM Brown.

10 | Setters at Work and Play

*T*he setter was developed for the express purpose of providing the hunter with a competent and reliable worker that could serve under the net and later under the gun in the pursuit and the retrieving of game. The setters, all of them, began as little more than tools for the sportsman, and it was a common assumption that the ability of the setter or any hunting dog would be compromised if the dog became a member of the family. Yet as time passed the owners of these useful dogs began to value the companionship of individual setters. Great men and women have been depicted in art and documented in the literature with a favorite Moll, Dash, Flo, Jeb or Bob. Even the admired old kennel managers, trainers, and gamekeepers at the castles and great estates had their favorites. On both sides of the Atlantic articles were written to assist owners in choosing a monosyllabic name and to offer advice on dog care in the home.

Today, there has been a resurgence of field interest and activities on the part of owners of all the "tribes" of setters. Also, new competitions have been introduced to provide owners with additional or alternative activities to show and field. Since its inception in 1934, Obedience Training competition has been extended to new and more complex competitions such as Agility Trials. A team competition for dogs has been introduced in the form of the Flyball Tournament. Most recently, special training and licensing have extended the use of setters in service to the ill, disabled and the elderly.

This chapter will address the roles that the setters play in the modern world. It will feature an article on setters in the field, and include sections on setters as companions, as participants in Obedience, Agility, Flyball, and therapy work, and as a breed with a long-standing and popular public image.

Setters In The Field

by Shelley P. LeBlanc and Joseph A. LeBlanc

We truly believe that setters—yes, even bench-bred setters—were meant to be both gun dogs and show dogs. And while our hearts skip a beat when any setter, regardless of pedigree, proportions or purpose, is on intense point, we know that we want it all—beauty and bird sense.

The purpose of this article, then, is to explain how interested setter owners can learn about, work toward, and know success in the field with the dog they have chosen. Areas of discussion will include: Beginning Young, New Horizons, Hunting Tests, and Dual Champions. Further, this article will focus on the fundamental relevance of criteria set forth in the breed standards to the performance of the ages-old work of setters in the bird field.

New England Fall Specialty Field Trial, 1950. Left to Right: Virginia Tuck, Jack Kilgus, Charlie Palmer, (?), Jim Smith, and Helen Kilgus.

Bench setters, for the most part, still have natural instincts for hunting. Most still have the desire to "get" the birds and many have a strong inclination to point game. The degree to which the hunting instincts exist in the four setters has not been studied. However, one method that can be used in selecting a bench-bred setter for use as a hunter is to examine the dog's pedigree and look for a title that designates a Hunt Test suffix or a Field Trial prefix.[1]

Retrieving, however, is the most difficult instinctive behavior to establish in today's setters. Therefore, once it has been observed that a setter has the desire to go after birds, retrieving is what should be introduced first. Keep in mind that this training is for the benefit of the hunter afoot and not for field trials or horseback handling; the goal is to prepare the setter to be a great hunting companion. It is essential that the dog learn the hunting game as a whole: the dog finds and points the bird, the trainer or owner flushes and shoots the bird, and the dog finds and retrieves the bird.

Beginning Young

When the puppy goes to its new home at about seven or eight weeks old, the owners should concentrate on one easy task: the retrieving game. Many new owners are concerned about whether the puppy will point, but that instinct is so strong that the first training should be in fetching. Owners can knot up an old sock and shut all the doors down a hallway so

the pup has nowhere to go except back to its owner. Playing fetch down the hallway must be introduced early on as a game. The setter puppy needs to know this as fun, and that it pleases the owner when the sock is retrieved. At the same time the "fetch" command is used, the "come" command should also be used. Both commands are necessary in the puppy's training regimen. The owner's voice as well as nonverbal behaviors such as facial expression, posture, arm and hand gestures, and ease of motion must be positive and unambiguous.

Keeping in mind that this is a youngster in body, brain, and attention span, make each session of the retrieving game short and sweet. Throw the sock a few times and observe the level of interest shown in the activity. When the interest wanes, end the "game" on a positive note. If this is the only thing that is taught in the session, the puppy will love the personal attention and will be less inclined to get bored.

When the puppy is doing well with the first skill, it is time to introduce the next step. Hold the puppy in a standing position while the object is thrown and use the command "whoa," which means it is not to move its legs. In giving the command "whoa", the owner is instructing the setter to wait while the bird flies. Incidentally, this vocabulary word, once learned, is also useful to settle the dog in the show ring and Obedience ring, and is a sound preparation for the AKC Hunt Tests which will be discussed later.

Once your puppy masters the skill of retrieving down the hallway, move it into a larger portion of your house, or outside if weather permits. At any rate, winter puppies in cold, harsh climates should not wait for spring to begin training. When more space is provided, however, the puppy should be controlled on a leash or a long check cord so that the owner can step on the cord or pull it in gently if it does not want to come on the retrieve. If the puppy learns early on that the owner is in control, it will not be so ready to challenge the process when it gets older.

A common mistake owners make when teaching retrieving is going after the pup to get the sock or object. This is a serious error. Rather, the owner should "play tag" with the puppy:

when the little setter starts in the direction of the owner, the owner should either backpedal or turn and run from the puppy so that it has to catch up. When the puppy catches the owner, it will be within easy reach to take back the object. This averts the common problem that occurs when the puppy approaches, but stops several feet away. When the owner takes the object from the puppy, the command "give" or "drop" can be given.

Another important training technique is not to take the object immediately, but to reward the puppy with praise and patting while the object is still in its mouth. After a few moments, the command to "give" or "drop" can be used.

When the puppy is three to four months old, it is advisable to introduce it to live birds. The earlier the puppy gets feathers and/or live birds into its mouth, the better. In fact, puppies can be introduced to birds earlier, but a wing or dead bird should be used prior to three months of age. Puppies, especially setter puppies, are more naturally curious and more willing at a young age to carry feathers in their mouths. If they are not exposed at an early age to having birds in the mouth, it can be very difficult to train dogs to retrieve. If they become accustomed to it early, training is much easier.

A constant, consistent, patient, and positive approach to training leads to success. The puppy should be challenged in small increments and enabled to succeed at each step. When the owner runs training sessions too long, or pushes too fast, or skips necessary steps, the whole training process will be impaired.

The following are examples of small steps. When the object is thrown six feet away and the pup is returning it with success, then throw it seven feet the next time or throw it around a corner so that it cannot be readily seen. A slightly more difficult game that can be played in the winter or during bad weather in warmer climes is hide and seek with a wing. Once the puppy is retrieving well, a wing can be thrown so that it is on the other side of the couch or even into an adjoining room. The next step is to put the puppy in another room, hide the wing and tell the puppy "dead bird." Encouraging the puppy to hit the ground using its nose to find the bird will be helpful in the future context of the bird field, and especially important when hunting birds such as ruffed grouse, which are very difficult to see after being shot.

Another example of a small step toward a greater challenge is when the puppy is retrieving on the lawn, and all training procedures are successful, move to an area of deeper grass at the edge of the lawn so the puppy will have to use its nose to find the wing or bird. In the future when you tell your dog "dead bird," it will know what to do because of that hide and seek game played as a puppy.

A third example of a small step is to introduce the wing together with the object or dummy to be thrown and retrieved. Or when the puppy is held and the "whoa" command is given, extend the waiting time before releasing the puppy to get the object or wing. Another advance along these lines is to put a leash on the puppy and take hands off when commanding it to "whoa." While it is important to keep the training fun and interesting by introducing new challenges, it is vital that each new step be undertaken only when the dog has demonstrated the prerequisite skills. Move to the next step only when you have every reason to believe that the dog can handle it. The goal is for the dog to succeed.

Goals to Achieve with the Young Setter

1. Bring out the natural instincts of the setter by exposing it to birds at a young age.

2. Have the pup come when called. This is done by always having control of the situation by the use of a check cord or a limited space so the puppy cannot run away.

3. The puppy should respond appropriately to the words fetch, come, give or drop, dead bird, and whoa.

4. Have the puppy retrieving live birds during the first live bird introduction. This is achieved after playing "retrieve" often and then moving to retrieving with feathers and finally to retrieving the live bird.

5. The puppy must have a firm idea of what "whoa" means and should obey that command well by the time birds are introduced. One note of caution here is that during early introductions to the live bird the puppy should not be discouraged by an immediate and/or firm use of "whoa" from getting the bird. Too early a "whoa" in the case of a live bird may discourage the puppy from developing a keen desire to get the bird.

Once the dog has shown "birdiness"—an interest in birds—and has been successful at carrying one in its mouth, then introduction to pointing can begin. A live bird is planted in moderate length grass so that it is easy for the puppy to find on the first try. Many puppies will come across the scent and naturally point the bird. If this happens, the owner should speak in a low and positive voice to the dog and go in and flush the bird. This introduction to pointing should not take place during a training session, but rather in a recreational context. Once the puppy has pointed, repeat the same procedure but with the addition of the noise of a cap gun or a blank gun that is not very loud. The gun should be fired when the puppy is at the height of the excitement of chasing the bird—usually at or just after the flush. If the owner has appropriately prepared for the sound of the gun, the puppy will probably not even hear the shot. For example, owners can shoot caps or blanks around the yard when the puppy is totally engrossed in an activity such as eating or playing. Especially if the noise of the gun at first comes from a distance, most puppies, unless they are very skittish, will not show much reaction to the gun. Still, it is often better if the gun is shot by someone else, who can be further away from the puppy. If the puppy does react in a negative way, the owner should use a reassuring voice and praise and comfort the puppy with words like, "It's okay." In any event, it is very important that the puppy be actively chasing the bird before the shot is fired.

It is also quite common that the puppy does not point a bird until it has had more opportunity to make a find. The owner should be patient and observe the puppy's behavior carefully. It is important for the owner to let the puppy develop the pointing behavior naturally. However, if, after a few birds have been planted and the puppy is still not pointing, the owner should plant the bird, and keeping a check cord on the puppy throughout the pointing exercise, lead the dog into the bird. When it seems the dog is catching some scent, gently tell the pup to "whoa" in a very soft and positive voice. Leading the way toward a skill for which the puppy has some instinct, and letting it know that this pleases the owner, are essential elements in the introduction to pointing.

Use of a check lead.

If the training sessions do not bring the puppy to pointing, the owner should stop for the day and try again on another day. Throughout this introductory phase the training sessions must be short, positive, and enjoyable. When the dog gets closer to a year old, greater expectations and corrections would be appropriate. Puppies need to be puppies. However, "come" is a given and the puppy must respond or correction is indicated. The one time when sharp correction is not advisable is when the puppy is working a bird.

During the hunting season the owner should take the puppy out and expose it to as much as its age, training time, and degree of skill allow it to handle. This experience must be one on one—puppy and owner—or a few hunters and the puppy. Never take the puppy out during the introductory period with a sizable group of people, dogs, guns or birds. Puppies can become confused and easily frightened by all the activity and noise, and naturally this is counter-productive to guiding the youngster toward being a gun dog.

New Horizons

Many owners who have focused primarily on showing the family setter find that they have an interest in introducing the dog to the field. Often the dog has finished its championship or Obedience degree, and the owner is seeking new activities to enjoy with the dog. The owner of an older setter should follow the same guidelines as presented in the "Beginning Young" section. Owners must prepare the dog by teaching the "come", "fetch", and "whoa" commands. This should be done before introducing the dog to live birds. It is not effective to teach commands when the dog is in contact with birds. Bird contact must be a positive experience.

If owners find that for a variety of reasons—time constraints, physical limitations, or other—they do not wish to continue with the dog's field training themselves, it is time to seek the help of a professional trainer. There are several factors to be considered. First, the owner should choose a trainer who has had experience with bench-bred setters and who has a positive attitude about the "show" setters' ability. Second, the owner should learn about the training methods of the professional trainer. It is advisable for the owner to participate in some short field sessions given by the trainer. The owner can observe the manner in which the dog is being handled and can have an opportunity to ask questions about further training methods. Third, the owner should ask for trainer recommendations from local setter club members, or setter fanciers who have some knowledge of field training. If the trainer is not found through word-of-mouth, it is important to get references, particularly in the case of setters going into advanced field training. The rate of progress will of course depend upon the dog's prior preparation, the dog's natural ability, and the appropriate "match" between the dog and the trainer. However, if the dog enters field training with little or no experience, there should be marked progress within a few weeks. If within a month even a dog without previous experience has not improved or looks skittish, then it is time to find a new trainer.

Dual Ch. Tartana Champagne Charlie CDG, MH. Photo by Wachuta.

American Kennel Club Hunt Tests

AKC Hunt Tests are field tests in which the dog is judged against a standard. Since they are non-competitive events, they ease newcomers into the sport without the stress of competition.

There are three levels of the hunt test program; Junior, Senior and Master. The Junior level is meant for young or less experienced dogs. The dogs have to be bold and independent in their search for game, they need to be generally obedient (the judges are usually pretty lenient for juniors) and they must find and point a bird (longer than a flash point) to pass the test. Junior Hunter braces normally last 20 minutes and the handlers use only a blank pistol. Live ammunition is not used in Junior tests. Junior dogs are judged in the following areas (American Kennel Club regulations for Hunting Tests for Pointing Breeds appear in italics):

1) Hunting—*must have a keen desire to hunt, show boldness and independence and have a fast, yet useful pattern of running.*

2) Bird Finding Ability—*must show intelligence in seeking objectives, use of the wind and the ability to find birds.*

3) Trainability—*this category includes the dog's willingness to be handled, reasonable obedience to commands and must show they are not gun shy when the blank gun is fired.*

4) Pointing—the dog must point a bird to pass the test. *The dog is judged on the intensity of its point, as well as its ability to locate (pinpoint) birds under difficult hunting conditions and/or confusing scent patterns. A "flash" point cannot be graded as pointing.*

Senior and Master Hunt Test braces generally last for 30 minutes. In this test qualified gunners use live ammunition to bring the birds down for the retrieve. A blank pistol is used if there is bird contact in the backfield.

Senior Hunt Test criteria are as follows:

1) *A Senior hunting dog must show all of the attributes expected of a Junior hunting dog in Hunting and Bird Finding Ability, but must be scored in these two categories with less tolerance than would be accorded to the Junior hunting dog.*

2) *A Senior hunting dog must point and hold its point until the bird has been shot or the dog has been released.*

3) *A Senior hunting dog must retrieve, but a dog need not deliver to hand.*

4) Trainability—in addition to the Junior hunt test requirements for this category, *a dog must stop on a wild flushed bird and may be commanded to do so.*

5) Honoring—*a Senior dog must honor* its bracemate's point.

Master Hunt Test criteria are as follows:

1) *A Master hunting dog must show all of the attributes of a Senior hunting dog in Hunting and Bird Finding Ability, but must exhibit these abilities in the more exceptional manner expected of a truly finished and seasoned hunting companion. Master hunting dogs must also possess all of the attributes of the Senior dog in Pointing, Retrieving, Trainability and Honoring.*

2) Pointing—*A Master hunting dog must be steady to wing and shot on all birds. A dog shall not be commanded to retrieve until positive steadiness has been demonstrated.*

3) Retrieving—*A dog cannot receive a qualifying score if it fails to deliver promptly, tenderly and absolutely to hand.*

4) Trainability—*The elements of handling and gun response are viewed more stringently in a Master hunting dog...A Master hunting dog must stop on a wild flushed bird without being given a command to do so. A dog that fails to do so, or a dog requiring a command to stop cannot receive a qualifying score.*

5) Honoring—*A Master hunting dog must honor; a dog requiring restraint, either physical or verbal, when honoring, or a dog that steals it's bracemate's point cannot receive a qualifying score.*

The Hunt Tests as they are described above provide goal levels for novice owners whose aim is to have a finished, polished gun dog. Many bench setter owners and their dogs have been introduced to the field by way of the Junior Hunt Test. Indeed, these owners are experiencing the magic that has been locked in the mind, the heart, and the nose of the setter for hundreds of years. And many setter owners who had never thought about hunting birds are now out in the fields working with their English, Gordon, and Irish Setters and they are enjoying the excitement of watching their setters do what they were born to do. (Although the Irish Red and White Setter may prove to be the most competent of the setters in the field in the future, the breed is not yet approved to compete in tests and trials in the United States.)

Irish Setter, Am. & Can. Ch. Windwood Autumn Tradition JH, CD, VC, CGC. Photo courtesy of Twistol and Seipkes.

Dual Champions and Triple Champions

A dual champion is a dog that has fulfilled the requirements for a show or bench championship and has also fulfilled the requirements for a field trial championship. A show dog must earn a total of fifteen points at AKC shows including two major wins where three, four or five points are awarded. The major wins must be earned under two different judges. A field champion must be recorded by the AKC as a Field Champion. A Triple Champion is a dog designated by the AKC as having completed a Champion of Record, Obedience Trial Champion and Field Champion.

The American Kennel Club requirements for Field Champion[2] are as follows:

> The setter must win "10 points ... in regular stakes in at least 3 licensed or member field trials, provided that 3 points have been won in one 3 point or better Open All-Age, Open Gun dog, Open Limited All-Age, or Open Limited Gun Dog stake, that no more than 2 points each have been won in Puppy and Derby Stakes, and that no more than 4 of the 10 points have been won by placing first in Amateur Stakes."

In order to compete for a Field Championship (FC), the handler may be either a professional or an amateur, while in competition for an Amateur Field Championship (AFC) the handler of the setter must be an amateur.

At field trials, as opposed to Hunt Tests, judges use a comparative and subjective set of criteria. In other words, the dogs are judged in comparison to the performance of other dogs in each prescribed event and the entries are evaluated by the perception of style as it exists in the mind of the judge. Further, judges look for ground race and speed. Dogs should cover a lot of ground and make a straight, fast course to the tree lines where the birds are located. Dogs must also move in a forward pattern without making the error of circling back behind the handler. Field trial dogs are expected to demonstrate an

Ch. Gordon Hill Sea Gem Sportster. Photo by Basham.

Mex. Am. Ch. Heathrows A Case of Blackmale JH, CGC. Photo by Samuelson.

Ch. Rice Creek's Cumulo Nimbus SH. Photo courtesy of LeBlanc.

assertive, confident and thoroughly outgoing attitude in the quest for game. They should also cover the terrain made available for the trial with thoroughness yet with thrift of motion.

Preparing the setter for field trial competition requires a more "hands off" approach than the preparation for the Hunt Tests. The young dog or puppy needs to learn early on to run hard and fast. Susan DeSilver, who has bred dual champion Gordon Setters, explains:

> When taking a young pup out with field trialing in mind, make every run special, from the beginning to the end. It is always a good idea to keep the puppy or youngster keenly interested in running and looking for those birds. Setting up a "break away" situation is also good exposure for a young pup. What this means is setting up an older dog on a "whoa", taking the pup with the lead on out of the vehicle or from behind a blind and, providing that puppy with a learning situation to point and back the other dog. If the youngster doesn't naturally back that dog on "whoa", gently put the puppy on a "whoa" and then unleash the youngster and blow the whistle—which means start

running hard to that first tree line! Running young dogs with older dogs that are more experienced, helps the young dog learn to run hard to the edges. Once the puppy or youngster points its own find, don't give it a lot of birds after that. It is important to create a pattern that makes the dog always focused and eager to look for those birds. This training will extend their range, which is imperative for a field trial setter. And as is true with any training procedure, always end before the dog slows down, shows diminished interest, or wants to quit.

"Hands off" means that there should be as little obedience training control as possible.

A field trial dog needs to be an aggressive, free and easy spirit. Overdoing the practice runs with heavy-handed training and control will hold the dog down, and this is exactly the opposite of what the judges are looking for. In fact, most of the training for a field trial dog is to encourage it to go out away from the handler. When training for steadiness on point for the gun dog stakes, hands off is a must in order to keep the style of the point up.

Photo by Fitzgerald.

Gordon Setter, FC Gordon Hill Leeward Ho. Photo by Basham.

DC/AFC Heathrow's Robbin'Hood, MH. Photo by Samuelson.

Gordon Setter, Australia, 1966. Photo courtesy of Ferguson.

There are field trials that do not require setters to retrieve the birds. Only the firing of a blank gun is used. This procedure in a field stake is very common on the East Coast and in the mid-west. On the West Coast retrieving stakes are very popular for the setters; unfortunately, however, the added dimension of training required for retrieving tends to limit or reduce the intensity and style of the performance of some setters. Whether or not retrieving should be part of the stake has been a hot topic of debate among field trialers. The simple solution is for the owner or handler to enter the type of field trial that is conducive to the training and natural abilities of the dog and the choices and expectations of the owner.

The Breed Standards and Setters in the Field

All four setter breeds were created to serve the hunter on foot. The standards describe the kind of dog that must be able to run, turn, and cover ground efficiently. Worthy setters found birds, pointed and retrieved. The range or distance from the hunter that the setter maintained was the result of training, the individual desire of the owner, and the abundance of game. Therefore, it can be argued that for today's bench-bred setter the best method of determining its practical worth is either the Hunt Test or the number of birds taken home for dinner.

DC Kelyric Starry Starry Sky, SH. Photo by Fitzgerald.

Yet over the years since the competition of field trials began, the speed of the pointing breeds including the setters has become an all-important criteria for judges, trainers, and handlers. Today, extreme importance is placed on ground race, speed, and style, and the dogs that have an advantage are the dogs that are bred specifically for this competition. The larger, heavier boned bench setters are at a disadvantage in this game. Although many are better balanced, work with less effort and are in many cases good endurance dogs, with fine bird finding ability, they are not capable of the speeds of the racier, leaner, smaller boned setters bred for the field.

For a bench bred setter to become a dual champion is a challenge. However, this challenge is being met by more setter owners than ever before. Today, all the setter breeds have numerous dual champions. While this is an exciting and meritorious achievement, setter fanciers who are planning to field trial a bench bred setter should be informed of the difficulty of their goal. First, as has already been discussed, there is the matter of speed. The setter will be competing not only against field trial bred setters, but may also be competing against the other pointing breeds such as pointers and shorthairs that are

His parents told him he was too little to handle a real dog in the ring.
Photo courtesy of Schepper.

known for speed. Second, the "style" most often deemed by the field judge as the criterion of excellence is a look of extreme intensity on point with a very high head and tail. The bench bred setter that meets the breed standard correctly does not have and should not have this high tail and is, thus seen by the judge as lacking in field trial style and intensity. Most field trial judges want to see a setter as exciting as it can be and the show setter in the trial with its larger body, horizontal tail, and fancy coat does not meet the judge's perception of "winner." Finally, there is the reality of cost for field trial competition. Fees for training, handling and board can be equal to or higher than those for show, especially in view of the duration of training away from home. Travel, equipment and entry fees are similar to show costs. Too often the novice owner's first impression of field competition is that it is more informal, casual and fun in the out of doors as compared to dog shows. It is also a common notion that because the field trial is judged on what a dog does rather than what a dog looks like, that the decisions are more objective. These first impressions are misleading. Field trial competition is taken just as seriously as show competition, and the level of objectivity in judging at trials depends largely on the judge.

Red & Whites at a Field Trial with Canon Doherty. Ireland.
Photo courtesy of Canon Doherty.

Today setters competing to earn a dual title face a dual problem. To be successful in the show ring, the dog must carry weight and coat similar to other well put down dogs. But weight and coat are difficult to maintain in the field. In fact, too much weight will slow the dog down and too much coat will get in the way or become damaged. Besides, the dog that is in hard muscle from field work will often be frowned upon by judges in the show ring; and the setter that has most often been successful in the field is at the middle or the lower end of the size called for in the breed standard, while show judges are likely to seek out the larger more substantial dog that remains within the standard.

In conclusion, the sport of setters in the field is where these breeds began, and an increasing interest in setters in the field is where we are today with our dogs. Through training and participation in the Hunt Tests, setters can prove their true heritage; and by going on to compete in field trials, today's setters can take a giant step beyond what they were originally bred to do.

Setters As Companions

The four setter breeds have proven over time that they make fine members of any family whether that family includes small children, growing youngsters, active teenagers, adults, or seniors. Setters have demonstrated that they have stable temperaments and can adjust and re-adjust to a variety of life styles. It is also common for setters to bond with different people in differing ways. They seldom "play favorites"; rather they enjoy and participate in many activities when the opportunity arises.

They were meant to be with people and they thrive on human relationships. The same dog can be gentle with a child, roughhouse with a teen, meet the working members of the family at the end of the day with excitement and provide the calm, reassuring companionship necessary for older owners.

Setters by nature are trustworthy in temperament. However, this ideal description of life with setters cannot be expected to happen without the guidance, patience and training by adult members of the family. Setters, as is true of all breeds, need to be socialized as puppies. They need to experience the sights and sounds of everyday life in a variety of places in order to establish a sound temperament. It is

*Photo courtesy of
Fitzgerald.*

Checking the property together at Our Lady of Mercy Church in New Jersey, Ch. Shabhin Bruno with Rev. Dan Herlihy, the vice-president of the Irish Red & White Setter Club of America.

important for the puppy to go out in public and learn the rules of public behavior. Outings should never be limited to a trip to the veterinarian. Puppies that are the only dogs in the family should also experience positive interaction with other dogs. In other words, setters need help growing up to be good canine citizens. They cannot be dependable as adult dogs if they are frightened or spooked by new situations. Many owners find local Obedience Training classes to be a helpful beginning in introducing the dog to the outside world. Breed and all breed clubs also offer Canine Good Citizen tests that are sponsored by the AKC.[3] These tests conducted by qualified evaluators include ten procedures that include accepting a friendly stranger, performing a sit and down on command, coming when called, and walking on a loose lead through a crowd. Dogs that pass the test have proven that they have the basic attributes necessary for being a dependable member of the family and in interactions with others beyond the family.

Furthermore, setters in a family must be treated in a responsible manner by all members of the family. Adults must provide careful supervision of their young children at play-time with the setter. Although setters are well known for their great patience with the sometimes harsh treatment by a toddler, no dog should ever have to endure discomfort at the hands of an unsupervised child. Dogs are not to be teased, poked, pulled, straddled or sat upon. These rules of behavior

*St. Patrick's Day
Parade, Somerville,
New Jersey. Photo
courtesy of Knoster.*

for children are fundamental to a child's appreciation and responsibility of becoming a dog owner.

Many times a family, after the loss of its beloved old pet that everyone remembers as canine perfection, goes out immediately and purchases a new puppy. And when the whining, biting, chewing, piddling little baby setter with more energy than a group of five-year-old children presents the family with unceasing demands and needs, the love affair with the newcomer becomes strained. It is difficult for any family to remember that old Duncan, Tess, Colleen, or Shannon ever acted like this. Furthermore, setter puppies grow very fast. Their legs are too long and their feet are too big, their mouths are always open in anticipation of a new treat or new experience and their busy setter tails are at just the right height to make a clean sweep of the coffee table. Wise owners provide the growing setter with training, guidance, and a regular activity before the setter becomes an unpleasant pet. Mrs.Maxwell[4] said it best, "setters need something to do."

Dogs and their owners share a wide variety of activities, and setters are involved in all of them. Whether in Obedience, Show, Junior Showmanship, Agility, hunting, field trials, Dog Therapy or even playing fetch or frisby in the back yard or park, setters are eager participants because it means sharing time with the people they like best.

Ch. Chandelle's Anchor Man with owner Joe Kaziny.

Setters In Obedience

The American Kennel Club's Obedience Regulations state, "The purpose of Obedience Trials is to demonstrate the usefulness of the pure-bred dog as a companion of people, not merely the dog's ability to follow specified routines in the obedience ring. The basic objective of Obedience trials is to produce dogs that have been trained and conditioned always to behave in the home, in public places, and in the presence of other dogs..." There are many levels of Obedience training[5] which can lead to competition at dog shows. But of primary importance is to provide training and activity for the setter so that it is a more useful, reliable and enjoyable pet.

Gordon Setter,
Ch. Pinebirch Rare
Review UD, JH, NA, NAJ.
Courtesy of McLatchy.

Irish Setter, Ch. Rapture's
Ring of Fire UD, JH, MX,
MXJ, VC, FM, C.G.C.
T.D.I., T.T.
Photo by Tien Tran
Photography.

Setters In Agility Trials And Flyball Tournaments

Agility Trials are offered by all-breed clubs and breed clubs as a competition that combines the speed and skill of the dog in a variety of progressively more difficult tests. This fast growing event is exciting to watch and it includes in its prescribed course such tests as the A-Frame, Dog Walks, See-Saws, jumps, and tunnels.

Irish Setter, photo by Tien Tran Photography.

Irish Red & White Setter, photo courtesy of Wallace-Jones.

Gordon Setter, photo courtesy of McLatchy.

Flyball tournaments are held separate from dog shows and are relatively new to dog competition. Dogs compete in relay teams with each dog running the course, releasing the flyball, and carrying it back to the finish line. These events employ sophisticated timing devices to decide the winners and competition is keen among dogs of breeds that are capable of fast starts, quick turns and speed on the right of way. Irish Setters in particular are physically and mentally adept at this type of competition. And they are not only effective at Flyball; since 1962 Irish Setter teams have demonstrated competence and have won at sled dog racing.

Irish Setter,
photo courtesy of Mertens.

Gordon Setter,
photo courtesy of McLatchy.

Irish Setter, Fire,
competing in Flyball.
Photo courtesy of Mertens.

Setters In Service As Therapy Dogs

Of all the activities discussed here, setters have demonstrated over many years that their steady and patient temperaments makes them particularly valuable in service as Therapy Dogs. Rosemary Bennett explains it this way:

> Therapy dogs and their handlers visit in many situations, from retirement homes to prisons. Some go to classrooms to talk to children about how to relate safely to dogs or how to care for their pets. Dogs and their owners with more experience can also work with physical therapists, psychologists and other health professionals to encourage a client to reach therapeutic goals. Several different organizations register or certify therapy dogs and their human partners. These can be international, national or local in scope. Many groups use the American Kennel Club's Canine Good Citizen test, either as it is written, or, with permission, in modified form, as part of their test.

Most add other scenarios to see if the dog is willing to be petted and handled by strangers of different ages and cultures. Evaluators may use medical equipment such as wheelchairs, walkers, and canes, offer treats, or create auditory or visual

Therapy Dog photos courtesy of Cora Hebert-Baboian.

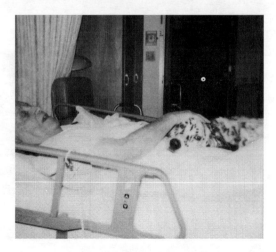

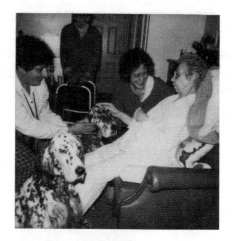

distractions. Distractions include things like dropped food or toys, loud noises, or someone shouting unexpectedly. Some groups have classes for the handlers. Most groups also require proof of vaccinations, and health screening forms which are filled out by the personal veterinarian. Generally, dogs and their handlers are expected to have good manners and social skills, to be reliable and non-threatening, and to enjoy people. Therapy dogs, especially setters, have made significant contributions to members of society who are in need.

Setters In The Public View

Although it was a Cocker Spaniel appearing in the New York production of the Barretts of Wimpole Street that renewed the American love affair with pure bred dogs, setters have always commanded public attention. They have graced the homes of the famous, appeared in stories and advertising, and performed on the stage as well as in front of the cameras. Daniel Webster and Henry Clay both had Gordon Setters, gifts from George W. Blunt.[6] An Irish Setter named Rufus H. Phelps[7] also known as the "red-headed Irishman" was dubbed 'the most literary dog in the world' because he greeted and spent time with such famous men of letters as George Bernard Shaw, Joseph Conrad, John Galsworthy, Hugh Walpole, and John Masefield when they visited in the home of Professor William Lyon Phelps at Yale University. When Rufus died at the age of fourteen in 1931, newspapers around the English speaking world reported the loss.

John James Audubon, the American naturalist is recorded as having an English Setter, even though the dog's likeness that appears in Davis Tuck's book is not entirely convincing. In fact, if the painting by Chappell were in color, it might be more evident that the dog carries characteristics of one of the other "tribes" of setter such as Red and White or black, white and tan. What is known, however, is that in the 1840's when Audubon was working on *Quadrupeds of America* with John Bachman, there were many imported setters and numerous native setters in the environs of New York City where he lived.

Nathaniel Currier and James Merritt Ives,[8] nineteenth century engravers, were famous for their popular renderings of American life. Of their numerous sporting prints, Irish Red and White Setter likenesses are clearly represented. It is particularly interesting to note that these setters are shown with a variety of game birds including duck and that the dogs are not the bright orange color that we now associate with the Welsh Springer, but rather the deeper hues of the setters from Ireland.

Famous as a Broadway musical comedy writer early in the twentieth century, William Cary Duncan also established

President Richard Nixon in the Oval Office with his dog Tirvelda King Timahoe and breeder Ted Eldredge. Official White House Photograph. Courtesy of Ann Eldredge Mateer.

Thistlerock Kennels the home of all three breeds of setters. He was the editor of *Outdoor Life*, a delegate to the American Kennel Club, and an avid field trial enthusiast.[9] Blue Mountain Plain Jane, grand dam of English Setter Ch. Sir Kip of Manitou, and owned by Dolores Klumbach, played for five years as one of Helen Keller's dogs in the Broadway play, The Miracle Worker.

Laura Delano, first cousin and confidante of Franklin Delano Roosevelt has long been associated with Irish Setters as a famous breeder and judge. Research recently reported by Doris Kearns Goodwin in *No Ordinary Time*[10] tells of an incident during WWII when the presidential train was on a sixteen-day trip through the deep South and Midwest. Of course the President's Scottish Terrier, Fala, was on board. But also present was Laura Delano's five-month-old Irish Setter puppy. According to documents by Tommy Thompson, "She (Laura) had to get off at every stop...find a grassy place and wait for (the puppy's) biological functions to occur." The secret service, operating under the most stringent security measures, were incensed one night to find the train in motion while Laura and her Irish Setter remained at a remote railway siding. Agents took immediate action throwing Laura up and over the retracted steps and threw the dog after her. Another Irish Setter had a more dignified relationship to an American president. King Timahoe, bred by Ted Eldredge, was the official White House pet of Richard Nixon and is shown here in the Oval Office after returning from a visit to Tirvelda farms in Virginia.

Everyone in America knew the face and form of the English Setter from the popular illustrations of Norman Rockwell, who also drew that charming picture of the Gordon and its master with the evening paper. The book *Raff, The Story of an English Setter* was the forerunner eclipsed by the book and then the movie, *Big Red*. Disney also included Raybar English Setters in the movie *The Biscuit Eater* and invited the California English Setter Club to a private showing. In Providence, Rhode Island in the 1960's Miss Bonnie of the *Romper Room* shared a WPRO TV "school room" with her students and her Irish Setter who was very adept at sampling the milk and cookies when the children with eyes tight shut were giving thanks for their snacks.

Bonnie Riker and her Irish Setter in the Romper Room. WPRO TV, Providence. Photo courtesy of Riker.

Irish Setter in a Woodie Wagon with permission by the Chrysler Corporation.

C.N. Myers of Blue Bar Kennels with Ch. Rip of Blue Bar.

Setters have been very popular dogs in advertising. Produce labels for *Setter Brand* had a wonderful painting of an English Setter, and alcoholic beverages have been sold in setter shaped bottles and marketed under the brand name *Old Setter*. Consumer items such as automobiles have used setters from promotion for many years. Chrysler Corporation photographed the most glamorous sports woman with the most glamorous sporting dog to advertise its Woody Wagon in 1947. Today, the Ford Motor Company has just published its advertisement for the vintage Thunderbird complete with an Irish Setter in the driveway. C.N. Myers, owner of the famous Blue Bar Kennels, posed with his favorite dog, Ch. Rip of Blue Bar for a dog food commercial. Setters from many kennels across the United States have also appeared on greeting cards and calendars.

However, the most splendid depiction of the setter in a public place is the fifteen foot tall bronze statue,[11] "Winds of Change," that stands in Irvine Park, California—a tribute to the generosity of James P. Irvine[12] (see back cover). The story of this man and this statue is an interesting one. Irvine's father came to America in 1849 as an immigrant from Ireland with "not a dollar in my pocket." With earnings from mining and a grocery business, the senior Irvine bought 110,000 acres of prime ranch land in what is now Orange County in Southern California. In 1886 the American-born James Irvine inherited the property which he eventually converted from ranch land to the most productive farmland in California. An avid sportsman, he hunted and fished on the land and established gun clubs for hunters. His kennel of Irish Setters was located on what is now Old Myford Road in Tustin near the family's picnic area and hunting preserve, which is now the public park that bears his name. As James Irvine donated the park land to the people of Orange County in 1897, his family donated the statue to commemorate the park's centennial[13] and to honor the man who with his setters always faced into the wind—the Santa Ana winds.

James Irvine and his Irish Setter.
(also see back cover for statue of James Irvine)
Photo permission by The First American Financial Corporation.

Endnotes

1   In studying a pedigree look for the following prefix and suffix titles to denote field capability. FC-Field Champion, AFC-Amateur Field Champion, NFC-National Field Champion, NAFC-National Amateur Field Champion. JH-Junior Hunter, SH-Senior Hunter, MH-Master Hunter.

2   http://www.akc.org/registration/rules/rftpnt.cfm?page=16.

3   http://www.akc.org/love/cgc/index.cfm.

4   C. Bede Maxwell, author of *The Truth About Sporting Dogs.* Published in 1972 by Howell Book House, Inc.

5   American Kennel Club Website http://www.akc.org.

6   Lloyd, Freeman. *All Setters Their Histories, Rearing and Training.* (Page 112-113).

7   Thompson, William C., *The New Irish Setter.* Howell Book House, 1976-Tenth Printing. (Page 59).

8   Nathaniel Currier, American Lithographer 1813-1888. James Merritt Ives, 1821-1895.

9   Thompson, William C., The New Irish Setter. (Page 59-61).

10   Page 425.

11   Bronze statue entitled *Winds Of Change* by Deborah Copenhaver. Photo by R. S. Brown.

12   http://www.irvine.org/about_irvine/history.html.

13   Taken directly from the inscription on the base of the statue.

Conclusion

$\mathscr{L}$ife long learning is not a concept exclusive to the college campus. It is alive and well among all kinds of people in the sport of dogs. During the process of writing this book I have communicated with setter people in the United States, Canada, England, Ireland, Germany and Australia. They have ranged in age from fourteen to ninety. They represent every imaginable occupation and profession. What they have in common is a sincere devotion to setters. Some have done what was thought to be impossible; this especially applies to the most stalwart who revived the fourth setter now known to us all as the Irish Red and White Setter. Many do not realize the merit of their continuing contributions. All have been gracious in meeting my requests, generous with their time and talents, and demonstrative of a willingness to go beyond what I dared to hope for. For me it has been a personal challenge and a responsibility that my mentors would have expected of me.

Although I am still concerned that readers will not want to address information that they do not agree with, I feel that I have a responsibility to share all that I have found out and not weaken my message by censorship. Indeed, if this book were to contribute nothing else to the setter breeds, I should be grateful if it led to a wider and more open discussion of the crucial role that breeders and judges play in delineating and enforcing the standards that identify our breeds—as they were, as they are, and as they will be.

I have been surprised by facts that although they relate only tangentially to the topic at hand, have peaked my curiosity. For example, I discovered that in both the old world and the

new, setters have benefitted from the devotion of a dispropor-
tionately high number of members of the clergy. I am
intrigued. Are they subtly aware of a beauty, a harmony, dare
one say a grace, that others are less naturally attuned to? And
how do they manage to fit Sunday services into the show and
field trial schedules?

Of course puzzles of a somewhat more serious nature will
have arisen from the research, and frustrations over photography continue to annoy. But this learning experience of mine
will, I hope, suggest new starting points for others who will
continue and expand the inquiry.

As I bring this book to a conclusion I can't help but reflect
on my beginning in the sport of dogs. Of the happy days spent
at Stone Gables with our setters in the practice ring. Of the late
nights whelping puppies and early mornings packing for a
show. Of the songs my sister and I sang with the Commander
to keep him awake and alert at the wheel on the way home
from dog shows. My memory of those days also includes
meeting Lydia, and Barbara and George in Children's Handling Classes. And I remember Morris and Essex as well as the
Teaneck Armory, Mechanic's Hall, and the Nutmeg Inn. And
of course I remember the Foley Boys. For me, the sport of dogs
has been a lifelong curriculum in humanity.

Appendix: Breed Standards

As explained in Chapter 7, The United States, Canada and The United Kingdom have different standards. Australia and New Zealand use the standard from The United Kingdom. The Federation Cynologique Internationale (FCI) is the governing body for Ireland, Europe and South America and uses the standard of the breeds' country of origin. The Irish Red and White Setter is not yet a recognized breed in the United States. Therefore, it is judged by the standards published by the Irish Red and White Setter Club of America and is shown under the rules of the American Rare Breeds Association.

Because standards are subject to revision the web address for access to the standards follows.

American Kennel Club: www.akc.org
Canadian Kennel Club: www.ckc.org
The Kennel Club (British): www.the-kennel-club.org.uk
Irish Kennel Club: www.ikc.org.ie
Federation Cynologique Internationale: www.fci.be
Irish Red and White Setter Club of America:
www.redandwhitesetter.org

American Kennel Club Standards
English Setter

General Appearance

An elegant, substantial and symmetrical gun dog suggesting the ideal blend of strength, stamina, grace, and style. Flat-coated with feathering of good length. Gaiting freely and smoothly with long forward reach, strong rear drive and firm topline. Males decidedly masculine without coarseness. Females decidedly feminine without over-refinement. Overall appearance, balance, gait, and purpose to be given more emphasis than any component part. Above all, extremes of anything distort type and must be faulted.

Head

Size and proportion in harmony with body. Long and lean with a well defined stop. When viewed from the side, head planes (top of muzzle, top of skull and bottom of lower jaw) are parallel. *Skull*—oval when viewed from above, of medium width, without coarseness, and only slightly wider at the earset than at the brow. Moderately defined occipital protuberance. Length of skull from occiput to stop equal in length of muzzle. *Muzzle*—long and square when viewed from the side, of good depth with flews squared and fairly pendant. Width in harmony with width of skull and equal at nose and stop. Level from eyes to tip of nose. *Nose*—black or dark brown, fully pigmented. Nostrils wide apart and large. *Foreface*—skeletal structure under the eyes well chiseled with no suggestion of fullness. Cheeks present a smooth and clean-cut appearance. *Teeth*—close scissors bite preferred. Even bite acceptable. *Eyes*—dark brown, the darker the better. Bright, and spaced to give a mild and intelligent expression. Nearly round, fairly large, neither deepset nor protruding. Eyelid rims dark and fully pigmented. Lids fit tightly so that haw is not exposed. *Ears*—set well back and low, even with or below eye level. When relaxed carried close to the head. Of moderate length, slightly rounded at the ends, moderately thin leather, and covered with silky hair.

Neck and Body

Neck—long and graceful, muscular and lean. Arched at the crest and cleancut where it joins the head at the base of the skull. Larger and more muscular toward the shoulders, with the base of the neck flowing smoothly into the shoulders. Not too throaty. *Topline*—in motion or standing appears level or sloping slightly downward without sway or drop from withers to tail forming a graceful outline of medium length. *Forechest*—well developed, point of sternum projecting slightly in front of point of shoulder/upper arm joint. *Chest*—deep, but not so wide or round as to interfere with the action of the forelegs. Brisket deep enough to reach the level of the elbow. *Ribs*—long, springing gradually to the middle of the body, then tapering as they approach the end of the chest cavity. *Back*—straight and strong at its junction with loin. *Loin*—strong, moderate in length, slightly arched. Tuck up moderate. *Hips*—croup nearly flat. Hip bones wide apart, hips rounded and blending smoothly into hind legs. *Tail*—a smooth continuation of the topline. Tapering to a fine point with only sufficient length to reach the hock joint or slightly less. Carried straight and level with the back. Feathering straight and silky, hanging loosely in a fringe.

Forequarters

Shoulder—shoulder blade well laid back. Upper arm equal in length to and forming a nearly right angle with the shoulder blade. Shoulders fairly close together at the tips. Shoulder blades lie flat and meld smoothly with contours of body. *Forelegs*— from front or side, forelegs straight and parallel. Elbows have no tendency to turn in or out when standing or gaiting. Arm flat and muscular. Bone substantial but not coarse and muscles hard and devoid of flabbiness. *Pasterns*—short, strong and nearly round with the slope deviating very slightly forward from the perpendicular. *Feet*—face directly forward. Toes closely set, strong and well arched. Pads well developed and tough. Dewclaws may be removed.

Hindquarters

Wide, muscular thighs and well developed lower thighs. Pelvis equal in length to and forming a nearly right angle with upper thigh. In balance with forequarter assembly. Stifle well bent and strong. Lower thigh only slightly longer than upper thigh. Hock joint well bent and strong. Rear pastern short, strong, nearly round and perpendicular to the ground. Hind legs, when seen from the rear, straight and parallel to each other. Hock joints have no tendency to turn in or out when standing or gaiting.

Coat

Flat without curl or wooliness. Feathering on ears, chest, abdomen, underside of thighs, back of all legs and on the tail of good length but not so excessive as to hide true lines and movement or to affect the dog's appearance or function as a sporting dog.

Markings and Color

Markings—white ground color with intermingling of darker hairs resulting in belton markings varying in degree from clear distinct flecking to roan shading, but flecked all over preferred. Head and ear patches acceptable, heavy patches of color on the body undesirable. *Color*—orange belton, blue belton (white with black markings), tricolor (blue belton with tan on muzzle, over the eyes and on the legs), lemon belton, liver belton.

Movement and Carriage

An effortless graceful movement demonstrating endurance while covering ground efficiently. Long forward reach and strong rear drive with a lively tail and a proud head carriage. Head may be carried slightly lower when moving to allow for greater reach of forelegs. The back strong, firm, and free of roll.

When moving at a trot, as speed increases, the legs tend to converge toward a line representing the center of gravity.

Size

Dogs about 25 inches; bitches about 24 inches.

Temperament

Gentle, affectionate, friendly, without shyness, fear or viciousness.

Approved November 11, 1986

Gordon Setter

General Appearance

The Gordon Setter is a good-sized, sturdily built, black and tan dog, well muscled, with plenty of bone and substance, but active, upstanding and stylish, appearing capable of doing a full day's work in the field. He has a strong, rather short back, with well sprung ribs and a short tail. The head is fairly heavy and finely chiseled. His bearing is intelligent, noble, and dignified, showing no signs of shyness or viciousness. Clear colors and straight or slightly waved coat are correct. He suggests strength and stamina rather than extreme speed. Symmetry and quality are most essential. A dog well balanced in all points is preferable to one with outstanding good qualities and defects. A smooth, free movement, with high head carriage, is typical.

Size, Proportion, Substance

Size—Shoulder height for males, 24 to 27 inches; females, 23 to 26 inches. Weight for males, 55 to 80 pounds; females, 45 to 70 pounds. Animals that appear to be over or under the prescribed weight limits are to be judged on the basis of conformation and condition. Extremely thin or fat dogs are discouraged on the basis that under or overweight hampers the true working ability of the Gordon Setter. The weight-to-height ratio makes him heavier than other Setters. *Proportion*—The distance from the forechest to the back of the thigh is approximately equal the height from the ground to the withers. The Gordon Setter has plenty of bone and substance.

Head

Head deep, rather than broad, with plenty of brain room. *Eyes* of fair size, neither too deep-set nor too bulging, dark brown, bright and wise. The shape is oval rather than round. The lids are tight. *Ears* set low on the head approximately on line with the eyes, fairly large and thin, well folded and carried close to the head. *Skull* nicely rounded, good-sized, broadest between the ears. Below and above the eyes is lean and the cheeks as narrow as the leanness of the head allows. The head should have a clearly indicated stop. *Muzzle* fairly long and not pointed, either as seen from above or from the side. The flews are not pendulous. The muzzle is the same length as the skull from occiput to stop and the top of the muzzle is parallel to the line of the skull extended. *Nose* broad, with open nostrils and black in color. The lip line from the nose to the flews shows a sharp, well-defined, square contour. *Teeth* strong and white, meeting in front in a scissors bite, with the upper incisors slightly forward of the lower incisors. A level bite is not a fault. Pitted teeth from distemper or allied infections are not penalized.

Neck, Topline, Body

Neck long, lean, arched to the head, and without throatiness. *Topline* moderately sloping. *Body* short from shoulder to hips. Chest deep and not too broad in front; the ribs well sprung, leaving plenty of lung room. The chest reaches to the elbows. A pronounced forechest is in evidence. Loins short and broad and not arched. Croup nearly flat, with only a slight slope to the tailhead. *Tail* short and not reaching below the hocks, carried horizontal or nearly so, not docked, thick at the root and finishing in a fine point. The placement of the tail is important for correct carriage. When the angle of the tail bends too sharply at the first coccygeal bone, the tail will be carried too gaily or will droop. The tail placement is judged in relationship to the structure of the croup.

Forequarters

Shoulders fine at the points, and laying well back. The tops of the shoulder blades are close together. When viewed from behind, the neck appears to fit into the shoulders in smooth, flat lines that gradually widen from neck to shoulder. The angle formed by the shoulder blade and upper arm bone is approximately 90 degrees when the dog is standing so that the foreleg is perpendicular to the ground. Forelegs big-boned, straight and not bowed, with elbows free and not turned in or out. Pasterns are straight. Dewclaws may be removed. Feet catlike in shape, formed by close-knit, well arched toes with plenty of hair between; with full toe pads and deep heel cushions. Feet are not turned in or out.

Hindquarters

The hind legs from hip to hock are long, flat and muscular; from hock to heel, short and strong. The stifle and hock joints are well bent and not turned either in or out. When the dog is standing with the rear pastern perpendicular to the ground, the thighbone hangs downward parallel to an imaginary line drawn upward from the hock. Feet as in front.

Coat

Soft and shining, straight or slightly waved, but not curly, with long hair on ears, under stomach and on chest, on back of the fore and hind legs, and on the tail. The feather which starts near the root of the tail is slightly waved or straight, having a triangular appearance, growing shorter uniformly toward the end.

Color and Markings

Black with tan markings, either of rich chestnut or mahogany color. Black pencilling is allowed on the toes. The borderline between black and tan colors is clearly defined. There are not any tan hairs mixed in the black. The tan markings are located as follows: (1) Two clear spots over the eyes and not over three-quarters of an inch in diameter; (2) On the sides of the muzzle. The tan does not reach to the top of the muzzle, but resembles a stripe around the end of the muzzle from one side to the other; (3) On the throat; (4) Two large clear spots on the chest; (5) On the inside of the hind legs showing down the front of the stifle and broadening out to the outside of the hind legs from the hock to the toes. It must not completely eliminate the black on the back of the hind legs; (6) On the forelegs from the carpus, or a little above, downward to the toes; (7) Around the vent; (8) A white spot on the chest is allowed, but the smaller the better. Predominantly tan, red or buff dogs which do not have the typical pattern of markings of a Gordon Setter are ineligible for showing and undesirable for breeding.

Gait

A bold, strong, driving free-swinging gait. The head is carried up and the tail "flags" constantly while the dog is in motion. When viewed from the front the forefeet move up and down in straight lines so that the shoulder, elbow and pastern joints are approximately in line. When viewed from the rear the hock, stifle and hip joints are approximately in line. Thus the dog moves in a straight pattern forward without throwing the feet in or out. When viewed from the side the forefeet are seen to lift up and reach forward to compensate for the driving hindquarters. The hindquarters reach well forward and stretch far back, enabling the stride to be long and the drive powerful. The overall appearance of the moving dog is one of smooth-flowing, well balanced rhythm, in which the action is pleasing to the eye, effortless, economical and harmonious.

Temperament

The Gordon Setter is alert, gay, interested, and aggressive. He is fearless and willing, intelligent and capable. He is loyal and affectionate, and strong-minded enough to stand the rigors of training.

DISQUALIFICATION

Predominantly tan, red or buff dogs which do not have the typical pattern of markings of a Gordon Setter.

Approved October 9, 1990
Effective November 28, 1990

OFFICIAL STANDARD OF
THE IRISH RED AND WHITE SETTER CLUB OF AMERICA, INC. 1997

*IRISH RED & WHITE SETTER

The following standard has been submitted to The American Kennel Club for application toward Miscellaneous Class status.

GENERAL APPEARANCE
Aristocratic, keen and intelligent. A large, red and white parti-colored bird dog with front of neck rough. A dog that is strong, powerful, well balanced and proportioned without lumber.

SIZE, PROPORTION, SUBSTANCE
Desirable height at withers, Males 24-1/2 to 26 inches. Bitches 22-1/2 to 24 inches. Body length, from point of shoulder to base of tail should never be shorter than height at point of shoulder. This setter should be well boned, muscular, with no tendency to fineness. A mature bitch may have less substance than a mature male.

HEAD
EXPRESSION - Soft expression of a bird dog.

EYES - Round and dark hazel or dark brown. May be slightly prominent, but show no haw. Pigment of rims may vary from dark pinkish brown to black. Well chiseled under eyes.

EARS - Set level with the eyes or above, lying close to the head; leather length should not reach past nose. It is a disqualification to alter coat on top of ears.

SKULL - Broad in proportion to body, occiput can be felt but not prominently seen. Should not be domed
or apple-headed.

STOP - Defined, but moderate rather than abrupt.

MUZZLE - Square. As long as skull. Slightly tapering from stop to nose. Parallel planes of skull and
muzzle are equally acceptable.

NOSE - Black or dark brown with well opened nostrils. Light spots on a dog under one year of age is acceptable.

LIPS - Not pendulous, but covers lower lips. Color black or dark brown.

BITE - The teeth should meet in a scissor bite. Wry, overshot or under-shot unacceptable. Level bite
acceptable.

NECK, TOPLINE AND BODY
NECK - Moderately long, very muscular, but not too thick. Slightly arched, free from all tendency to
throatiness. It is a disqualification to alter the Coat on front of neck.

TOPLINE - A straight, slightly sloping line from withers to base of tail.

BODY (PARTS)
    BACK - Very muscular and powerful
    CHEST - Deep, reaching the elbow on a mature dog.
    RIBS - Rounded, but not barrel chested.
    LOIN - Muscular and short rather than long.
    TUCKUP - Is definite, but not exaggerated.
    CROUP - Very slight drop in croup.
    TAIL - Moderate length, well feathered with no appearance of ropi-ness. Set on nearly level with the croup as a natural extension of the topline, strong at root, tapering to end. Carriage straight or curved slightly upward, nearly level with the back.

FOREQUARTERS
    SHOULDERS - Well laid back. Forearm and upper arm should be relatively equal in length and form a ninety-degree angle at point of shoulder.
    ELBOWS - Free, turning neither in nor out.
    FORELEGS - Straight and sinewy, well boned.
    DEWCLAWS - Are usually removed.
    PASTERNS - Should be strong.
    FEET - Round, closely knit, with plenty of featherings between toes.
    NAILS - Are kept short and may be black, dark brown or light colored.

HINDQUARTERS

LEGS - As viewed from the rear are wide and powerful. From hip to hock should be long and muscular; from hock to heel of moderate length.

STIFLE AND HOCK JOINTS - Are angulated and turning neither in nor out

DEWCLAWS - If any should be removed.

FEET - Same as front.

COAT

On head, front of legs and tips of ears, short and fine; on other parts of the body and legs moderate length, flat and free from curl but slight wave permissible, with the following exceptions: Feather on upper portion of ears long and silky; on back of fore and hind legs long and fine; fair amount of hair on belly, forming fringe, which extends onto chest and throat. All feathering straight and flat.

It is a disqualification to alter the coat on the top of ears or front of neck. Bottom of feet including edges may be cleared of hair. Pasterns and hocks may be thinned for neatness. Light trimming allowed under base of tail for cleanliness. No other trimming is allowed including the whiskers which are to remain untrimmed.

COLOR

Parti-colored; the base color white with red patches. The white should be a pure white and the red should be a deep chestnut red, the darker the better. Flecking permitted around the face and feet and up the foreleg as far as the elbow and up the hindleg as far as the hock. Roaning, flecking and mottling on any other part of the body not desirable.

GAIT

At a trot, gait long striding, very lively, graceful and efficient. Head held high, hindquarters drive smoothly and with great power. Forelegs reach well ahead and yet remain low. Seen from front or rear, forelegs and hindlegs below the hock joint move perpendicular to the ground with some tendency toward a single track as speed increases. Crossing or weaving of legs, front or back is very objectionable.

TEMPERAMENT

Displays a kindly, friendly attitude behind which should be a discernible determination, courage and high spirit.

DISQUALIFICATION

Any alteration of coat on top of ears or front of neck.

Irish Setter

General Appearance

The Irish Setter is an active, aristocratic bird dog, rich red in color, substantial yet elegant in build. Standing over two feet tall at the shoulder, the dog has a straight, fine, glossy coat, longer on ears, chest, tail and back of legs. Afield, the Irish Setter is a swift-moving hunter; at home, a sweet natured, trainable companion. At their best, the lines of the Irish Setter so satisfy in overall balance that artists have termed it the most beautiful of all dogs. The correct specimen always exhibits balance, whether standing or in motion. Each part of the dog flows and fits smoothly into its neighboring parts without calling attention to itself.

Size, Proportion, Substance

There is no disqualification as to size. The make and fit of all parts and their overall balance in the animal are rated more important. 27 inches at the withers and a show weight of about 70 pounds is considered ideal for the dog; the bitch 25 inches, 60 pounds. Variance beyond an inch up or down is to be discouraged. *Proportion*—Measuring from the breastbone to rear of thigh and from the top of the withers to the ground, the Irish Setter is slightly longer than it is tall. *Substance*—All legs sturdy with plenty of bone. Structure in the male reflects masculinity without coarseness. Bitches appear feminine without being slight of bone.

Head

Long and lean, its length at least double the width between the ears. Beauty of head is emphasized by delicate chiseling along the muzzle, around and below the eyes, and along the cheeks. *Expression* soft, yet alert. *Eyes* somewhat almond shaped, of medium size, placed rather well apart, neither deep set nor bulging. Color, dark to medium brown. *Ears* set well back and low, not above level of eye. Leather thin, hanging in a neat fold close to the head, and nearly long enough to reach the nose. The *skull* is oval when viewed from above or front; very slightly domed when viewed in profile. The brow is raised, showing a distinct stop midway between the tip of the nose and the well-defined occiput (rear point of skull). Thus the nearly level line from occiput to brow is set a little above, and parallel to, the straight and equal line from eye to nose. *Muzzle* moderately deep, jaws of nearly equal length, the underline of the jaws being almost parallel with the top line of the muzzle. *Nose* black or chocolate; nostrils wide. Upper lips fairly square but not pendulous. The *teeth* meet in a scissors bite in which the upper incisors fit closely over the lower, or they may meet evenly.

Neck, Topline, Body

Neck moderately long, strong but not thick, and slightly arched; free from throatiness and fitting smoothly into the shoulders. *Topline* of body from withers to tail should be firm and incline slightly downward without sharp drop at the croup. The *tail* is set on nearly level with the croup as a natural extension of the topline, strong at root, tapering to a fine point, nearly long enough to reach the hock. Carriage straight or curving slightly upward, nearly level with the back. *Body* sufficiently long to permit a straight and free stride. *Chest* deep, reaching approximately to the elbows with moderate forechest, extending beyond the point where the shoulder joins the upper arm. Chest is of moderate width so that it does not interfere with forward motion and extends rearwards to well sprung ribs. *Loins* firm, muscular and of moderate length.

Forequarters

Shoulder blades long, wide, sloping well back, fairly close together at the withers. Upper arm and shoulder blades are approximately the same length, and are joined at sufficient angle to bring the elbows rearward along the brisket in line with the top of the withers. The elbows moving freely, incline neither in nor out. *Forelegs* straight and sinewy. Strong, nearly straight pastern. *Feet* rather small, very firm, toes arched and close.

Hindquarters

Hindquarters should be wide and powerful with broad, well developed thighs. Hind legs long and muscular from hip to hock; short and perpendicular from hock to ground; well angulated at stifle and hock joints, which, like the elbows, incline neither in nor out. Feet as in front. Angulation of the forequarters and hindquarters should be balanced.

Coat

Short and fine on head and forelegs. On all other parts of moderate length and flat. Feathering long and silky on ears; on back of forelegs and thighs long and fine, with a pleasing fringe of hair on belly and brisket extending onto the chest. Fringe on tail moderately long and tapering. All coat and feathering as straight and free as possible from curl or wave. The Irish Setter is trimmed for the show ring to emphasize the lean head and clean neck. The top third of the ears and the throat nearly to the breastbone are trimmed. Excess feathering is removed to show the natural outline of the foot. All trimming is done to preserve the natural appearance of the dog.

Color

Mahogany or rich chestnut red with no black. A small amount of white on chest, throat or toes, or a narrow centered streak on skull is not to be penalized.

Gait

At the trot the gait is big, very lively, graceful and efficient. At an extended trot the head reaches slightly forward, keeping the dog in balance. The forelegs reach well ahead as if to pull in the ground without giving the appearance of a hackney gait. The hindquarters drive smoothly and with great power. Seen from front or rear, the forelegs, as well as the hind legs below the hock joint, move perpendicularly to the ground, with some tendency towards a single track as speed increases. Structural characteristics which interfere with a straight, true stride are to be penalized.

Temperament

The Irish Setter has a rollicking personality. Shyness, hostility or timidity are uncharacteristic of the breed. An outgoing, stable temperament is the essence of the Irish Setter.

Approved August 14, 1990
Effective September 30, 1990

Canadian Kennel Club Standards

English Setter

General Appearance
An elegant, stylish and symmetrical gun dog of good substance that projects a heritage of well developed hunting instinct and bird sense. He suggests the ideal blend of strength and stamina combined with grace and style. Flat-coated with feathering of adequate length. Gaiting freely and smoothly with long forward reach and strong rear drive. Males should be decidedly masculine in appearance without coarseness. Females should be decidedly feminine in appearance without over-refinement.

Temperament
A true gentleman by nature, he has a kind and gentle expression and is constantly expressing a willingness to please with an affectionate, happy and friendly attitude. He has a lovable, mild disposition and is without fear or viciousness.

Size
Dogs about 25 inches (63cm); bitches about 24 inches (61cm) in height, when measured at the withers. Symmetry—the balance of all parts to be considered. Symmetrical dogs will have level toplines or will be slightly higher at the shoulders than at the hips. They will have well-angulated fore and rearquarters that work smoothly together. Balance harmony of proportion, elegance, grace and an appearance of quality, substance, and endurance to be looked for.

Coat
The coat should be flat without curl or wooliness. The dog should be adequately feathered on the ears, the chest, the belly, the underside of the thighs, the back of all legs and on the tail. The feathering, however, should not be so excessive that it hides the true lines and movement of the dog, nor should it affect the dog's appearance or function as a sporting dog.

Colour
Black and white, orange and white, liver and white, lemon and white, white, black-white and tan, orange belton, liver belton, lemon belton, tricolour belton, blue belton. The belton markings may vary in degree from clear, distinctive flecking to roan shading. Dogs without heavy patches of colour on the body, but flecked all over preferred.

Head & Skull
The entire head should be in proportion to the body. It should be long and lean with a well-defined stop. **Skull:** when viewed from above, should be oval. The skull should be of medium width, without coarseness, and should be only slightly wider at the base than at the brows. The widest part of the oval should be at the ear set. There should be a moderately defined occipital protuberance. The length of the skull from the occiput to the stop should be equal in length to the muzzle. **Muzzle:** brick-shaped and the width to be in harmony with the skull. It should be level from the eyes to the tip of the nose. When viewed from the side, the line of the top of the muzzle should be parallel to the line of the top of the skull. A dish face or a Roman nose is objectionable. The flews should be square and pendant. The **nose** to be black or dark brown in colour except in white, orange and white, lemon and white or liver and white where it may be lighter. The nostrils should be wide apart and large in the openings. **Foreface:** the skeletal structure under the eyes should be well chiseled with no suggestion of fullness. The cheeks, like the sides of the muzzle, should present a smooth and clean-cut appearance. **Jaws:** The lower jaw should extend in length so that the lower teeth form a close scissors bite with the upper teeth. The inner surface of the upper teeth in contact with the outer surface of the lower teeth when the jaws are closed. An even bite is not objectionable. The **teeth** should be

strongly developed with upright incisors. Full dentition is desirable. **Eyes** should be bright, and the expression mild and intelligent. The iris should be brown, the darker the better. The eyelid rims should be fully pigmented. **Ears** should be set low and well back. Preferably, the set should be even with the eye level. When relaxed, the ears should be carried close to the head. They should be of moderate length, slightly rounded at the ends, and covered with long silky hair.

Neck

The neck should be rather long, muscular, and lean. The neck should be slightly arched at the crest and clean-cut where it joins the head at the base of the skull. The neck should be larger and very muscular toward the shoulders, and the base of the neck should flow smoothly into the shoulders. The neck should not be too throaty or pendulous and should be graceful in appearance.

Shoulder

The shoulder blade (scapula) should be laid back to approach the ideal angle of 45 degrees from the vertical. The upper foreleg (humerus) should be equal in length to the shoulder blade (scapula) and form an angle of 90 degrees with the shoulder blade. This enables the elbow to be placed directly under the back edge of the shoulder blade and bring the heel pad directly under the pivot point of the shoulder thus giving a maximum length of stride. The shoulders should be fairly close together at the tips, but with sufficient width between the blades to allow the dog to easily lower its head to the ground. The shoulder blades should lie flat and meld smoothly with the contours of the body. This structure permits perfect freedom of action for the forelegs.

Forelegs

When seen standing from the front or side, the forelegs or arms (radius and ulna) should be straight and parallel. The elbows should nave no tendency to turn either in or out when standing or gaiting. The upper arm (humerus) should be flat and muscular. The bone should be fully developed and muscles hard and devoid of flabbiness. The pastern should be short, strong, and nearly round with the slope from the pastern joint to the foot deviating very slightly forward from the perpendicular.

Feet

The feet should be closely set and strong, pads well developed and tough; toes well arched and protected with short, thick hair.

Forechest

The forechest should be well developed, and the point of the sternum (prosternum) should project about 3/4 - 1 inch (2 - 3 cm) in front of the point of the shoulders.

Rib Cage
The chest should be deep, but not so wide or round as to interfere with the action of the forelegs. The keel should be deep enough to reach the level of the elbow. The ribs should be long, springing gradually to the middle of the body, then tapering as they approach the end of the thoracic cavity.

Topline
The topline of the body of the dog in motion or standing should appear to be level or to slope very slightly from the withers to the tail forming a graceful outline of medium length without sway or drop. The tail should continue as a smooth, level extension of the topline.

Back
The back, the area between the withers and the loin, should be straight and strong at its junction with the loin area. The loins should be strong, moderate in length, slightly arched, but not to the extent of being roached or wheel-backed, and only discernible to the touch.

Hips
The slope and length of the croup determines the tail-set, and the degree of slope should not be more than 15 degrees from the horizontal for an ideal tail-set. The hip bones should be wide apart with the hips nicely rounded and blending smoothly into the hindlegs. The pelvis should slope at an angle or 30 degrees from the horizontal. The pelvis governs the forward reach and the backward follow-through of the hind legs, and this angle permits a maximum length of stride. Again for efficiency and balance, the length of the pelvis and the upper thigh (femur) should be equal, and they in turn should be equal in length to the shoulder blade (scapula) and upper arm (humerus).

Hind Legs
The upper thigh (femur) should be well developed and muscular. The well-developed lower thigh (tibia/fibula) in a well-balanced setter should be slightly longer than the upper thigh (femur) and should become wide and flat as it approaches the hock joint. The knee joint (stifle) should be well bent and strong. The pastern from the hock joint to the foot, should be short, strong, and nearly round and perpendicular when viewed from the side. The hind legs, when seen from the rear, should be straight and parallel to each other and the hock joints should have no tendency to turn in or out either at rest or when the dog is in motion.

Tail
The tail should be straight and taper to a fine point with only sufficient length to reach the hock joint or less. The feather must be straight and silky, hanging loosely in a fringe and tapering to a point when the tail is

raised. There must be no bushiness. The tail should not curl sideways or curl above the level of the back (sickle tail).

Gait

An effortless graceful movement demonstrating rapidity and endurance while covering the ground efficiently. There must be a long forward reach and strong rear drive with a lively tail and a proud head carriage. Head may be carried slightly lower when moving to allow for greater reach of the forelegs. The back of the dog should remain strong, firm, and level when in motion. When moving at a trot, the properly balanced dog will have a tendency to converge toward a line representing the centre of gravity of the dog.

Faults

1. Any deviation from the affectionate, happy, friendly attitude which makes the English Setter the true gentleman of the dog world.
2. Undershot or overshot bite.
3. Any dog over 27 inches (69 cm) or under 24 inches (61 cm). Any bitch over 26 inches (66 cm) or under 23 inches (58 cm).
4. Incorrect tail set or a tail carriage such as a steep drop from the hips to the tail set or a tail which curls sideways or curls above the level of the back (sickle tails).
5. Incorrect soft and woolly coat texture that will not protect the dog while working in the field.
6. Light eyes. Loose eyes.
7. A lack of long forward reach and strong rear drive.
8. A hackneyed, paddling gait and a rolling, stilted, or lumbering motion.
9. Flat, splayed, or long feet or feet that turn in or out.
10. Too narrow or too wide a front.
11. Barrel-like or slab-sided rib cage.
12. A down-faced or snipey muzzle.
13. Flews in excess of that required to present a square muzzle.
14. A lack of back skull.
15. Cow-hocks.
16. Any deviation from a topline that is level or very slightly sloping.

GORDON SETTER

General Appearance

A good-sized, sturdily built dog, well muscled, with plenty of bone and substance, but active, upstanding and stylish, appearing capable of doing a full day's work in the field. Strong, rather short back, well-sprung ribs and short tail, a fairly heavy head, finely chiseled, intelligent, noble and dignified expression, showing no signs of shyness; clear colours and straight of slightly waved coat. A dog that suggests strength and stamina rather than extreme speed.

Symmetry and quality are most crucial. A dog well balanced in all points is preferable to one with outstanding good qualities and defects.

Size

Shoulder height for males, 24-27 inches (61-69 cm); for females, 23-26 inches (58-66 cm).

Weight: Males, 55-75 lb. (25-34 kg); Females, 45-65 lb. (20-29 kg).

As a guide, the greater heights and weights are to be preferred provided that character and quality are also combined. Dogs over and under these heights and weights are to be discouraged.

Coat and Colour

Coat should be soft and shining, resembling silk, straight or slightly waved - the later preferred - but not curly, with long hair on ears, under stomach, on chest, and on back of the fore and hind legs to the feet. Deep, shining coal-black with tan markings, either of rich chestnut or mahogany red colour. The tan should be shining and not dull, yellowish or straw colour and not mixed with black hairs. Black penciling allowed on toes. The borderlines between black and tan colours should be clearly defined. There should not be any tan colours mixed in the black.

Tan markings:

(a) Two clear spots over the eyes not over 3/4 inch (2 cm) in diameter.

(b) On the sides of the muzzle, the tan should not reach above the base of nose, resembling a stripe around the end of the muzzle from one side to the other.

(c) On the throat.

(d) Two large, clear spots on chest.

(e) On the inside of the hind legs and inside of thighs showing down the front of the stifle and broadening out to the outside of the hind legs from the hock to the toes. It must, however, not completely eliminate the black on the back of hind legs.

(f) On the forelegs from the knees or a little above downward to the toes.

(g) Around the vent.

A white spot on the chest is allowable, but the smaller the better.

Head
Deep rather than broad, with plenty of brain room, nicely rounded good-sized skull, broadest between the ears. The head should have a clearly indicated stop. Below and above the eyes should be lean and the cheek as narrow as the leanness of the head allows. The **muzzle** fairly long with almost parallel lines and not pointed either as seen from above or from the side. The flews not pendulous but with clearly indicated lips. The **nose** big, broad with open nostrils and of black colour. **Eyes** of fair size, neither too deep set nor too bulging, dark brown, bright and wise. **Ears** set low on the head, fairly large and thin.

Neck
Long, lean, arched to the head and without throatiness.

Forequarters
Shoulders should be fine at the points, deep and sloping well back, giving a moderately sloping topline. Forelegs big-boned, straight, not bowed either in or out, with elbows free, well let down and not inclined either in or out.

Body
Chest deep and not too broad in front; the ribs well sprung, leaving plenty of lung room.

Hindquarters
The hind legs from hip to hock should be long, flat, and muscular, from hock to heel short and strong. The stifle and hock joints well bent, and not inclined either in or out. Both fore and hind feet should have close knit, well-arched toes with plenty of hair between with full toe pads and deep heel cushions.

Tail
Short and should not reach below the hocks, carried horizontal or nearly so, thick at the root and finishing in a fine point. The feather, which starts near the root of the tail, should be slightly waved or straight and have a three-square appearance growing shorter uniformly toward the end.

Gait
A smooth free movement with high head carriage.

Faults
1. General Impression - Unintelligent appearance. The Bloodhound type with heavy and big head and ears and clumsy body, as well as the Collic type with its pointed muzzle and curved tail, or showing any signs of shyness.
2. Head - Houndy, pointed, snipey, drooping or upturned muzzle, too small or large mouth.
3. Eyes - Too light in colour, too deep-set, or too prominent.

4. Ears - Set too high or unusually broad or heavy.
5. Neck - Thick and short.
6. Shoulders and Back - Irregularly formed.
7. Chest - Too broad.
8. Legs and feet - Crooked legs. Out-turned elbows. The toes scattered, flat-footed.
9. Tail - too long, badly carried or hooked at the end.
10. Coat - Curly like wool, not shining.
11. Colour - Yellow or straw coloured tan or without clearly defined lines between the different colours. White feet. Too much white on the chest. In the black there must be no tan hairs which can appear often around the eyes.

IRISH RED AND WHITE SETTER

General Appearance
Strong and powerful, well balanced and proportioned without lumber; athletic rather than racy.

Temperament
Aristocratic, keen and intelligent. Displays a kindly, friendly attitude, behind which should be discernible determination, courage and high spirit.

Size
Desirable height at withers:
Dogs: 24 1/2 inches to 26 inches (62 to 66 cm.)
Bitches: 22 1/2 inches to 24 inches (57 to 61 cm.)

Coat and Colour
Hair: long, silky, fine hair called "feathering" on the back of the fore and hind legs and on the outer ear flap, also a reasonable amount on the flank extending on to the chest and throat forming a fringe. All feathering straight, flat and not over profuse. The tail should be well feathered. On the head, front of legs and other parts of the body the hair should be short, flat and free from curl but slight wave is permissible.
Base colour white with solid red patches (clear islands of red colour), both colours should show the maximum of life and bloom; flecking but not roaning permitted around the face and feet and up the foreleg as far as the elbow and up the hind leg as far as the hock; roaning, flecking and mottling on any other part of the body is most objectionable and is to be heavily penalized.

Head
Broad in proportion to the body. **Skull:** domed without showing occipital protuberance, as in the Irish Red Setter. **Stop:** good stop. **Muzzle:**

clean and square. **Jaws:** of equal or nearly equal length. **Teeth:** regular; scissors bite ideal; level bite acceptable. **Eyes:** dark hazel or dark brown; round, with slight prominence and without haw. **Ears:** Set level with the eyes, and well back, lying close to the head.

Neck
Moderately long, very muscular, but not too thick, slightly arched, free from all tendency to throatiness.

Forequarters
Forelegs straight and sinewy, well boned. Shoulders well laid back. Elbows free, turning neither in nor out. Pastern strong.

Body
Strong and muscular. Back very muscular and powerful. Chest, deep with well sprung ribs.

Hindquarters
Wide and powerful; hind legs from hip to hock long and muscular, from hock to heel of moderate length and strong. Stifle well bent. Hock well let down, turning neither in nor out. Feet close knit with plenty of feathering between toes.

Tail
Moderate length, not reaching below hock, strong at root, tapering to a fine point; no appearance of ropiness and carried level with or below the back.

Gait
When moving at the trot long striding, very lively, graceful and efficient. Head held high, hindquarters drive smoothly and with great power. Forelegs reach well ahead and remain low. Seen from front or rear forelegs and hind legs below the hock joint moving perpendicularly to the ground; no crossing or weaving of legs, front or back.

Faults
Any departure from the foregoing points should be considered a fault and the seriousness with which the fault should be regarded should be in exact proportion to its degree.

N.B.: Male animals should have two apparently normal testicles fully descended into the scrotum.

IRISH SETTER

General Appearance

The Irish Setter is an active, aristocratic bird-dog, rich red in colour, substantial yet elegant in build. Standing over two feet tall at the shoulder, the dog has a straight, fine, glossy coat, longer on ears, chest, tail and back of legs. Afield, he is a swift-moving hunter; at home, a sweet-natured, trainable companion. He is a rollicking personality. At his best the lines of the Irish Setter satisfy in over-all balance that artists have termed him the most beautiful of all dogs. The correct specimen always exhibits balance whether standing or in motion. Each part of the dog flows and fits smoothly into its neighbouring parts without calling attention to itself.

Size

There is no disqualification as to size. The make and fit of all parts and their over-all balance in the animal are rated more important. A height of 27 inches (69 cm) at the withers with a show weight of about 70 lb. (32 kg) is considered ideal for a dog; the bitch, 25 inches (64 cm), 60 lb. (27 kg). Variance beyond 1 inch (3 cm) up or down to be discouraged.

Coat and Colour

Short and fine on head, forelegs and tips of ears; on all other parts, of moderate length and flat. Feathering long and silky on ears, on back of forelegs and thighs long and fine, with a pleasing fringe of hair on belly and brisket extending onto the chest. Feet well feathered between the toes. Fringe on tail moderately long and tapering. All coat and feathering as straight and free as possible from curl or wave. Colour: mahogany or rich chestnut red, with no trace of black. A small amount of white on chest, throat, or toes, or a narrow centred streak on skull, is not to be penalized.

Head

Long and lean, its length at least double the width between the ears. The brow is raised, showing a distinct stop midway between the tip of the nose and well-defined occiput (rear point of skull). Thus the nearly level line from occiput to brow is set a little above, and parallel to, the straight and equal line from eye to nose. **Skull** is oval when viewed from above or front; very slightly domed when viewed in profile. Beauty of head is emphasized by delicate chiseling along the muzzle, around and below the eyes, and along the cheeks. **Muzzle** moderately deep, nostrils wide, jaws, of nearly equal length. Upper lips fairly square but not pendulous, the underline of the jaws being almost parallel with the topline of the muzzle. **Nose** black or chocolate. The **teeth** meet in a scissors bite evenly. **Eyes** somewhat almond-shaped, of medium size, placed rather well apart; neither deep-set nor bulging. Colour: dark to medium brown. Expression soft yet alert. **Ears** set well back and low, not above level of eye. Leather thin, hanging in a neat fold close to the head, and nearly long enough to reach the nose.

Neck

Moderately long, strong but not thick, and slightly arched; free from throatiness, and fitting smoothly into the shoulders.

Forequarters

Shoulder blades long, wide, sloping well back, fairly close together at the top and joined in front to long upper arms angled to bring the elbows slightly rearward along the brisket. Forelegs straight and sinewy, the elbows moving freely. All legs sturdy, with plenty of bone, and strong, nearly straight pasterns.

Body

Sufficiently long to permit a straight and free stride. Topline of body from withers to tail slopes downward without sharp drop at the croup. Chest deep, reaching approximately to the elbows; rather narrow in front. Ribs well sprung. Loins of moderate length, muscular, and slightly arched.

Hindquarters

Hindquarters should be wide and powerful with broad, well-developed thighs. Hind legs long and muscular from hip to hock, short and nearly perpendicular from hock to ground; well angulated at stifle and hock joints, which, like the elbows, incline neither in nor out. Feet rather small, very firm, toes arched and close.

Tail

Strong at root, tapering to fine point, about long enough to reach the hock. Carriage straight or curving slightly upward, nearly level with the back.

Gait

At the trot the gait is big, very lively, graceful and efficient. The head is held high. The hindquarters drive smoothly and with great power. The forelegs reach well ahead as if to pull in the ground, without giving the appearance of a hackney gait. The dog runs as he stands—straight. Seen from the front or rear, the forelegs, as well as the hind legs below the hock joint, move perpendicularly to the ground, with some tendency towards a single track as speed increases. But a crossing or weaving of the legs, front or back, is objectionable.

The Kennel Club (British)

ENGLISH SETTER

General Appearance
Of medium height, clean in outline, elegant in appearance and movement.

Characteristics
Very active with a keen game sense.

Temperament
Intensely friendly and good natured.

Head and Skull
Head carried high, long and reasonably lean, with well defined stop. Skull oval from ear to ear, showing plenty of brain room, a well defined occipital protuberance. Muzzle moderately deep and fairly square, from stop to point of nose should equal length of skull from occiput to eyes, nostrils wide and jaws of nearly equal length, flews not too pendulous; colour of nose black or liver, according to colour of coat.

Eyes
Bright, mild and expressive. Colour ranging between hazel and dark brown, the darker the better. In liver beltons only, a lighter eye acceptable. Eyes oval and not protruding.

Ears
Moderate length, set on low, and hanging in neat folds close to cheek, tip velvety, upper part clothed in fine silky hair.

Mouth
Jaws strong, with a perfect, regular and complete scissor bite, i.e. upper teeth closely overlapping lower teeth and set square to the jaws. Full dentition desirable.

Neck
Rather long, muscular and lean, slightly arched at crest, and clean-cut where it joins head, towards shoulder larger and very muscular, never throaty nor pendulous below throat, but elegant in appearance.

Forequarters
Shoulders well set back or oblique, chest deep in brisket, very good depth and width between shoulder blades, forearms straight and very muscular with rounded bone, elbows well let down close to body, pasterns short, strong, round and straight.

Body
Moderate length, back short and level with good round widely sprung ribs and deep in back ribs, i.e. well ribbed up.

Hindquarters
Loins wide, slightly arched, strong and muscular, legs well muscled
including second thigh, stifles well bent and thighs long from hip to
hock, hock inclining neither in nor out and well let down.

Feet
Well padded, tight, with close well arched toes protected by hair
between them.

Tail
Set almost in line with back, medium length, not reaching below hock,
neither curly nor ropy, slightly curved or scimitar-shaped but with no
tendency to turn upwards: flag or feathers hanging in long pendant
flakes. Feather commencing slightly below the root, and increasing in
length towards middle, then gradually tapering towards end, hair long,
bright, soft and silky, wavy but not curly. Lively and slashing in movement and carried in a plane not higher than level of back.

Gait/Movement
Free and graceful action, suggesting speed and endurance. Free movement of the hock showing powerful drive from hindquarters. Viewed
from rear, hip, stifle and hock joints in line. Head naturally high.

Coat
From back of head in line with ears slightly wavy, not curly, long and
silky as is coat generally, breeches and forelegs nearly down to feet well
feathered.

Colour
Black and white (blue belton), orange and white (orange belton), lemon
and white (lemon belton), liver and white (liver belton) or tricolour, that
is blue belton and tan or liver belton and tan, those without heavy
patches of colour on body but flecked (belton) all over preferred.

Size
Height: dogs: 65-69 cms (251/2-27 ins); bitches: 61-65 cms (24-251/2 ins).

Faults
Any departure from the foregoing points should be considered a fault
and the seriousness with which the fault should be regarded should be
in exact proportion to its degree.

Note
Male animals should have two apparently normal testicles fully
descended into the scrotum.

September 2000

Copyright The Kennel Club. Reproduced with their kind permission.

GORDON SETTER

General Appearance
Stylish dog, with galloping lines. Consistent with its build which can be compared to a weight-carrying hunter. Symmetrical in conformation throughout.

Characteristics
Intelligent, able and dignified.

Temperament
Bold, outgoing, of kindly even disposition.

Head and Skull
Head deep rather than broad, but broader than muzzle, showing brain room. Skull slightly rounded, broadest between ears. Clearly defined stop, length from occiput to stop slightly longer than from stop to nose. Below and above eyes lean, cheeks as narrow as leanness of head allows. Muzzle fairly long with almost parallel lines, neither pointed, nor snipy. Flews not pendulous, clearly defined lips. Nose large, broad, nostrils open and black. Muzzle not quite as deep as its length.

Eyes
Dark brown, bright. Neither deep nor prominent, set sufficiently under brows, showing keen, intelligent expression.

Ears
Medium size, thin. Set low, lying close to head.

Mouth
Jaws strong with a perfect, regular and complete scissor bite, i.e. upper teeth closely overlapping lower teeth and set square to the jaws.

Neck
Long, lean, arched, without throatiness.

Forequarters
Shoulder blades long, sloping well back, wide flat bone, close at withers, not loaded. Elbows well let down, and close to body. Forelegs flat-boned, straight, strong; upright pasterns.

Body
Moderate length, deep brisket, ribs well sprung. Back ribs deep. Loins wide, slightly arched. Chest not too broad.

Hindquarters
From hip to hock long, broad and muscular, hock to heel short, strong, stifles well bent, straight from hock joint to ground. Pelvis tending to horizontal.

Feet
Oval, close-knit, well arched toes, plenty of hair between. Well padded toes, deep heel cushions.

Tail
Straight or slightly scimitar, not reaching below hocks. Carried horizontally or below line of back. Thick at root, tapering to fine point. Feather or flag starting near root, long, straight, growing shorter to point.

Gait/Movement
Steady, free-moving and true, with plenty of drive behind.

Coat
On head, front of legs, tips of ears short and fine, moderate length; flat and free from curl or wave on all other parts of body. Feather on upper portion of ears long and silky; on backs of legs long, fine, flat and straight, fringes on belly may extend to chest and throat. As free as possible from curl or wave.

Colour
Deep, shining coal black, without rustiness, with markings of chestnut red, i.e. lustrous tan. Black pencilling on toes and black streak under jaw permissible. 'Tan markings': two clear spots over eyes not over 2 cms (3/4 in) in diameter. On sides of muzzle, tan not reaching above base of nose, resembling a stripe around clearly defined end of muzzle from one side to other. Also on throat, two large, clear spots on chest. On inside hindlegs and inside thighs, showing down front of stifle and broadening out to outside of hindlegs from hock to toes. On forelegs, up to elbows behind, and to knees or little above, in front. Around vent. Very small white spot on chest permissible. No other colour permissible.

Size
Height: dogs: 66 cms (26 ins); bitches: 62 cms (241/2 ins). Weight: dogs: 29.5 kgs (65 lbs); bitches: 25.5 kgs (56 lbs).

Faults
Any departure from the foregoing points should be considered a fault and the seriousness with which the fault should be regarded should be in exact proportion to its degree.

Note
Male animals should have two apparently normal testicles fully descended into the scrotum.

March 1994

IRISH RED and WHITE SETTER

General Appearance
Strong and powerful, without lumber; athletic rather than racy.

Characteristics
Biddable, highly intelligent, good worker.

Temperament
Happy, good-natured and affectionate.

Head and Skull
Head broad in proportion to body, with good stop. Skull domed without occipital protuberance as in Irish Setters, fairly square, clean muzzle.

Eyes
Hazel or dark brown, round, slight prominence, and without haw.

Ears
Set level with eyes and well back, lying close to head.

Mouth
Jaws strong with a perfect regular scissor bite, i.e. upper teeth closely overlapping lower teeth and set square to the jaws.

Neck
Moderately long, very muscular, but not too thick, slightly arched, free from throatiness.

Forequarters
Shoulders well laid back. Elbows free, turning neither in nor out. Strong, oval bone, well muscled, sinewy, pasterns slightly sloping.

Body
Strong and muscular, deep chest and well sprung ribs. Back and quarters very muscular and powerful. Bone strong, well built up with muscle and sinew.

Hindquarters
Wide and powerful. Legs from hip to hock long and muscular from hock to heel short and strong. Stifle well bent, hocks well let down turning neither in nor out.

Feet
Close-knit, well feathered between toes.

Tail
Strong at root, tapering to fine point, with no appearance of ropiness; not reaching below hock. Well feathered, carried level with back or below in lively manner.

Gait/Movement
Long, free-striding, effortless with drive.

Coat
Finely textured with good feathering. Slight wave permissible but never curly.

Colour
Clearly particoloured, i.e. base colour pearl white, solid red patches. Mottling or flecking but no roaning permitted around face and feet and up foreleg to elbow and up hindleg to hock.

Faults
Any departure from the foregoing points should be considered a fault and the seriousness with which the fault should be regarded should be in exact proportion to its degree.

Note
Male animals should have two apparently normal testicles fully descended into the scrotum.

March 1994

Copyright The Kennel Club. Reproduced with their kind permission.

IRISH SETTER

General Appearance
Must be racy, balanced and full of quality. In conformation, proportionate.

Characteristics
Most handsome, and refined in looks, tremendously active with untiring readiness to range and hunt under any conditions.

Temperament
Demonstrably affectionate.

Head and Skull
Head long and lean, not narrow or snipy, not coarse at the ears. Skull oval (from ear to ear) having plenty of brain room and well-defined occipital protuberance. From occiput to stop and from stop to tip of nose to be parallel and of equal length, brows raised showing stop. Muzzle moderately deep, fairly square at end. Jaws of nearly equal length, flews not pendulous, nostrils wide. Colour of nose dark mahogany, dark walnut or black.

Eyes
Dark hazel to dark brown, not too large, preferably like an unshelled almond in shape, set level (not obliquely), under brows showing kind, intelligent expression.

Ears
Of moderate size, fine in texture, set on low, well back and hanging in a neat fold close to head.

Mouth
Jaws strong, with a perfect, regular and complete scissor bite, i.e. upper teeth closely overlapping lower teeth and set square to the jaws.

Neck
Moderately long, very muscular but not too thick, slightly arched and free from all tendency to throatiness, setting cleanly without a break of topline into shoulders.

Forequarters
Shoulders fine at points, deep and sloping well back. Forelegs straight and sinewy having plenty of bone, with elbows free, well let down and not inclined either in or out.

Body
Chest as deep as possible, rather narrow in front. Ribs well sprung leaving plenty of lung room and carried well back to muscular loin, slightly arched. Firm straight topline gently sloping downwards from withers.

Hindquarters
Wide and powerful. Hindlegs from hip to hock long and muscular, from hock to heel short and strong. Stifle and hock joints well bent and not inclined either in or out.

Feet
Small, very firm; toes strong, close together and arched.

Tail
Of moderate length proportionate to size of body, set on just below the level of the back, strong at root tapering to a fine point and carried as nearly as possible on a level with or below the back.

Gait/Movement
Free flowing, driving movement with true action when viewed from front or rear, and in profile, showing perfect co-ordination.

Coat
On head, front of legs and tips of ears, short and fine; on all other parts of body and legs of moderate length, flat and as free as possible from curl or wave. Feathers on upper portion of ears long and silky; on back of fore- and hindlegs long and fine. Fair amount of hair on belly, forming

a nice fringe which may extend on to chest and throat. Feet well feathered between toes. Tail to have fringe of moderately long hair decreasing in length as it approaches point. All feathering to be as straight and flat as possible.

Colour
Rich chestnut with no trace of black. White on chest, throat, chin or toes, or small star on forehead or narrow streak or blaze on nose or face not to disqualify.

Faults
Any departure from the foregoing points should be considered a fault and the seriousness with which the fault should be regarded should be in exact proportion to its degree.

Note
Male animals should have two apparently normal testicles fully descended into the scrotum.

March 1994

Copyright The Kennel Club. Reproduced with their kind permission.

Irish Kennel Club
Federation Cynologique Internationale uses the breed standards from the country of origin.

Irish Red and White
UTILIZATION: Most acceptable companion and friend in the home and in the field. The Irish Red & White Setter is bred primarily for the field. The standard as set out hereunder must be interpreted chiefly from this point of view and all Judges at bench shows must judge the exhibits chiefly from the working standpoint.

GENERAL APPEARANCE: Strong well balanced and proportioned without lumber; athletic rather than racy. The Irish Red & White Setter is bred primarily for the field and must be judged chiefly from the working standpoint.

BEHAVIOUR/TEMPERAMENT: Aristocratic, keen and intelligent. Displays a kindly, friendly attitude, behind which should be discernible determination, courage and high spirit. The Red and White Setter is a very friendly, dependable and easily trained gundog.

PHYSICAL CHARACTERISTICS HEAD: Broad in proportion to the body.

CRANIAL REGION: Skull: Domed without showing occipital protuberance, as in the Irish Red Setter. Stop: Good Stop.

FACIAL REGION: Muzzle: Clean and square. Jaws: Jaws of equal or nearly equal length; Teeth: Regular teeth; scissor bite ideal; edge to edge bite acceptable. Eyes: Dark hazel or dark brown; round, with slight prominence and without haw. Ears: Set level with the eyes, and well back, lying close to the head.

NECK: Moderately long, very muscular, but not too thick, slightly arched, free from all tendency to throatiness. BODY: Strong and muscular. Back: To be strong and well muscled. Chest: Deep, with well sprung ribs.

TAIL: Moderate length, not reaching below hock, strong at root. Tapering to fine point; no appearance of ropiness and carried level with or below the back. LIMBS Legs well muscled and sinewy; strong bone.

FOREQUARTERS: Shoulders: Well laid back. Elbows: Free, turning neither in nor out. Forelegs: straight and sinewy, well boned. Pastern: Strong.

HINDQUARTERS: Wide and strong, hind legs from hip to hock long and muscular. Stifle: Well bent. Hock: Well let down, turning neither in nor out, from hock to heel of moderate length and strong.

FEET: Close-knit with plenty of feathering between toes.

GAIT/MOVEMENT: When moving at the trot long striding, very lively, graceful and efficient. Head held high, hindquarters drive smoothly and with great power. Forelegs reach well ahead and remain low. Seen from front or rear forelegs and hindlegs below the hock joint moving perpendicularly to the ground, no crossing or weaving of legs, front or back.

COAT HAIR: Long silky fine hair called "Feathering" on the back of the fore and hind legs and on the outer ear flap, also a reasonable amount on the flank extending on to the chest and throat forming a fringe. All feathering straight, flat and free from curl but slight wave is permissible. The Tail should be well feathered. On all other parts of the body the hair should be short, flat, and free from curl.

COLOUR: Base colour white with solid red patches (clear islands of red colour), both colours should show the maximum of life and bloom; flecking but not roaning permitted around the face and feet and up the foreleg as far as the elbow and up the hindleg as far as the hock; roaning, flecking and mottling on any other part of the body is most objectionable and is an eliminating fault.

SIZE: (Height) Desirable height at withers: Dogs 24 1/2 - 26 ins (62-66cm) Bitches 22 1/2 - 24 ins (57-61cm)

FAULTS Any departure from the foregoing points should be considered a fault and the seriousness with which the fault should be regarded should be in exact proportion to its degree.

SEVERE FAULTS: Any dog or bitch not conforming to the height standard

ELIMINATING FAULTS: Although flecking but not roaning is permitted around the face and feet and up the forelegs as far as the elbow and up the hindleg as far as the hock: roaning, flecking and mottling on any other part of the body is most objectionable and is an eliminating fault. Males not having two apparently normal testicles. Dogs showing aggression.

NOTE: Male animals should have two apparently normal testicles fully descended into the scrotum.

Irish Setter

UTILIZATION: Gun dog and family dog.

GENERAL APPEARANCE: Racy and athletic full of quality, kindly in expression. Balanced and in proportion.

BEHAVIOUR-TEMPERAMENT: Keen, intelligent, energetic, affectionate and loyal.

PHYSICAL CHARACTERISTICS HEAD: Long and lean, and not coarse at the ears. Muzzle and skull of equal length and on parallel lines

CRANIAL REGION: Skull: Oval (from ear to ear), having plenty of brain room, and with well defined occipital protuberance. Brows raised. Stop: Well defined.

FACIAL REGION: Nose: The colour of the nose is dark mahogany, or dark walnut or black, the nostrils wide. Muzzle: Moderately deep and fairly square at the end. From the stop to point of nose, long, flews not pendulous. Jaws: Jaws of nearly equal length. Teeth: Scissors bite. Eyes: Dark hazel or dark brown ought not to be too large. Ears: Of moderate size, fine in texture, set low and well back, hanging in a neat fold close to head.

NECK: Moderately long, very muscular, not too thick, slightly arched, no tendency to throatiness.

BODY: Proportionate to size of dog. Chest: Deep chest reaching the elbow, rather narrow in front, ribs well sprung, leaving plenty of lung room. Loins: Muscular and slightly arched.

TAIL: Moderate length, proportionate to size of body, set on rather low, strong at root, tapering to fine point. Carried level with or elbow back.

LIMBS FOREQUARTERS: Shoulders Fine at the point, deep and sloping well back. Elbows: Free and well let down, not turned in or out. Forelegs: Straight and sinewy, well boned.

HINDQUARTERS: Wide and powerful. Hindlegs: Long and muscular from hip to hock; from hock to heel short and strong. Stifle: Well bent Hocks: turned neither in or out.

FEET: Small, very firm, toes strong, arched and close together.

GAIT/MOVEMENT: Free flowing, driving movement; head held high. Forelegs reaching well ahead but carried low. Hindquarters drive smoothly with great power. Crossing or weaving of legs unacceptable.

COAT HAIR: On head, front of legs, and tips of ears, short and fine; on other parts of body and legs moderate length, flat and as free as possible from curl or wave. Feather on upper portion of ears along and silky; on back of fore and hind legs long and fine; fair amount of hair on belly, forming fringe which may extend onto chest and throat. Feet well feathered between toes. Tail having fringe of moderately long hair, decreasing in length as it approaches the point. All feathering straight and flat.

COLOUR: Rich chestnut with no trace of black; white on chest, throat, and toes; or small star on forehead or narrow streak or blaze on nose of face not to disqualify.

SIZE Height) Height at withers Males 23ins (58 cm) to 26.5 ins (67 cm) Female 21.5(55cm) to 24.5 (62 cm)

NOTE: Male animals should have two apparently normal testicles fully descended into the scrotum.

FAULTS: Any departure from the foregoing points should be considered a fault and the seriousness of the fault should be in exact proportion to its degree.

ADDENDUM
It is proposed over the next twelve (12) years to standardise the height to a range of 23 ins. (58.4 cm) and to 26.5 ins (67.3 cm) for males and 21.5 ins (54.6 cm) to 24.5 ins (62.2 cm) for females. During this period, setters that are balanced and in proportion, but outside the commended height ranges should not be penalised. The following interim targets are set: -Year 2002 Males 23 ins to 27 ins (58.5 to 68.5 cm) Females 20.5 ins to 25.5 ins. (52.00 to 64.75cm) Year 2006 Males 23 ins to 27 ins (58.5 to 68.5 cm) Females 21 ins to 25 ins. (53.5 to 63.5 cm)

Bibliography

An Illustrated Standard for The Irish Red & White Setter. The Irish Red & White Setter Club of America, Inc., 1996.

Barnes, Margaret. *English Setters Ancient and Modern.* Muffin Books, 1982. England.

Bepler, M. Ingle and Ryan, C.W. *Setters Irish, English, and Gordon.* "Our Dogs" Publishing Co., 1937. England.

Brigden, Patricia. *The Irish Red and White Setter.* Biddles Ltd, Guildford and King's Lynn, 1990. England.

Brown, Curtis. *Dog Locomotion and Gait Analysis.* Hoflin Publishing Ltd., 1986.

Brown, Curtis and Thelma. *The Art and Science of Judging Dogs.* B & E Publications, Inc., 1976.

Brown, Marsha Hall and Mason, Bethny Hall. *The New Complete Junior Showmanship Handbook.* Howell Book House, Inc., 1986.

Clark, Anne Rogers, Interview with. September 2001.

Classic American Homes. November 2001. Hearst Corporation, New York, NY.

DeFoix, Gaston. *Livre de Chase,* English translation, Edward, 2nd Duke of York, 1406-1413. (Modern translation, Chatto and Windus, 1909) (In Maxwell).

Dog News. September 1990. Harris Publications, New York, NY.

Eldredge, E. Irving and Vanacore, Connie. *The New Complete Irish Setter.* Howell Book House, Inc., 1983.

English Setter Association of America (English Setter Annuals).

Forsyth, Jane Kamp, Interview with. September 2001.

Gardner, E. *Irish Setters Today,* 1998. Ringpress, Lydney UK.

Gentry, Daphne. *Dog Art.* The American Kennel Club Dog Museum, St. Louis, 1996.

Goodwin, Doris Kearns. *No Ordinary Time.* Simon & Schuster, 1994 (pg. 425).

Gordon Setter Club of America Review 1978-1988. The Gordon Setter Club of America, Inc., 1990.

305

Gordon Setter Review 1989-1995. The Gordon Setter Club of America, Inc., 1997.

Gronowski, Ann. *Dogs in Sport/Dogs at Play.* The American Kennel Club Museum of the Dog, St. Louis, 1998.

Hall, Virginia Tuck, Interview with. September 2001.

Herendeen, Charles, Interview with. September 2001.

Hubbard, C.L.B. *The English Setter Handbook,* 1958. Nicholson & Watson, London.

Humphrey, Curtis. *The Irish Red & White Setter.* Curtis Humphrey, 2000.

Hutchinson, Lieut.-Gen. W.N. *Dog Breaking,* 1869. John Murray, London.

Hutchinson, W., (editor). *Dog Encyclopedia,* 1935. Hutchinson, London.

Idstone. *The Dog.* Cassell, Petter, Galpin & Co., 1872. England.

Laverack, Edward. *The Setter.* Longmans, Green, and Co., 1872. England.

Lee, Rawdon B. *Modern Dogs (Sporting).* Horace Cox, 1893. England.

Leighton-Boyce, Gilbert. *A Survey of Early Setters.* Leighton-Boyce, 1985. England.

Lloyd, Freeman. *All Setters Their Histories, Rearing and Training.* Freeman Lloyd, 1931.

Look, Jean Sanger and Lustenberger, Anita. *The Complete Gordon Setter.* Howell Book House, Inc., 1984.

Maxwell, C. Bede. *The Truth about Sporting Dogs.* Howell Book House, Inc., 1972. Also published in England.

Nichols, Virginia Tuck. *How to Show Your Own Dog.* The Practical Science Publishing Company, 1956.

Nielsen, John, Interview with. June 2000.

Nilsen, Joyce, Interview with. February 1999.

Official National Pictorial 1975 edited by Bernard and Wilma Baron. Published by the *Irish Setter Club of America, Inc.*

Phillips, W. Enos. *The True Pointer and His Ancient Heritage.* Phillips, W. Enos, 1970.

Popular Dogs Magazine. Popular Dogs Publishing Company, George F. Foley, Publisher. Philadelphia, PA United States. Reference Copies 1962-1972.

Pure-Bred Dogs American Kennel Gazette. American Kennel Club, Inc., New York, NY.

Shaw, Vero. *Illustrated Book of the Dog.* London, Cassell, 1890.

Shields, Jeannette Brady, Interview with. September 2001.

Spira, Harold R. *Canine Terminology.* Harper & Row Publishers, 1982. Australia. Also published in United States by Howell Book House.

Stonehenge and American writers. *The Dogs of Great Britain, America, and Other Countries.* Orange Judd Co., 1885.

The AKC's World of the Pure-Bred Dog, The American Kennel Club. Howell Book House, Inc., 1983.

The Irish World: The Art and Culture of the Irish People. Harrison House/ Harry N. Abrams, Inc., New York,1986.

Thompson, William C. *The New Irish Setter.* Howell Book House, Inc., 1976.

Trotter, William R., Interview with. August, 2001.

Tuck, Davis. *The Complete English Setter.* Denlinger's, 1951.

Tuck, Davis. *The New Complete English Setter.* Howell Book House, 1964.

Visualizations of the Dog Standards. Howell Book House, Inc., 1975 and 1977.

Watson, James. *The Dog Book.* Doubleday, Page & Co., 1909.

World of Setters, The. May/June 1972. Hollywood, CA.

Index